BETTE MIDLER

Rob Baker

CORONET BOOKS
Hodder and Stoughton

First published in the United States by
Fawcett Publications, Inc.

Coronet edition 1980

_____

Printed in Great Britain for Hodder and
Stoughton, Ltd., Mill Road, Dunton Green,
Sevenoaks, Kent (Editorial Office: 47
Bedford Square, London, WC1 3DP) by
Richard Clay (The Chaucer Press) Ltd,
Bungay, Suffolk

ISBN 0 340 25327 4

BETTE MIDLER

Finally! A book that tells it all — the whole uncensored story of superstar Bette Midler. A total intimate look at the Divine Miss M — her youth in Hawaii, her start in 'gay' baths, her meteoric climb to the top of the pop charts, and TV and movie stardom — plus the forces that shaped her and the people who helped her.

BETTE MIDLER
a little lady with a great big heart — and even more nerve

for peter

acknowledgments

For their kind cooperation: Bill Hennessy, Charlotte Crossley, Sharon Redd, Robin Grean, Gail Kantor, André de Shields, Cheryl Hardwick, Billy Cunningham, Lewis Friedman, Buddy Fox, Eliot Hubbard, Steve Ostrow, William Duff-Griffin, Peter Dallas, Budd Friedman, Bruce Vilanch, Linda Hopkins, Marta Heflin, Rosalie Mark, Albert Fullerton, Tony Finstrom, Louis Miele, Peter Born, Jon Philips, Candy Leigh, Patrick Cochrane, and Ula Hedwig.

To Larry Paulette, for permission to look through his 25-pound shopping bag of Midler clippings.

To the courteous employees of the Rodgers and Hammerstein Archives of Recorded Sound at the New York Public Library's Lincoln Center branch.

To Joe Glin, Nancy Moore, Joan Pikula, Albert Fullerton, William Kosmas, Gus Ginnochio and Henry Post for looking over the manuscript (and for general moral support).

To Jasper Jones of Popular Library, who encouraged me to write this book.

contents

back at the baths again

A fairly large crowd had gathered on the sidewalk in front of the Luxor Baths on West 46th Street in New York, including a healthy number of young would-be actors, singers, and dancers from the city-run High School of Performing Arts across the street.

"What's going on?" a newcomer asked, eying the sound cables and lighting equipment spread all over the sidewalk and the bored-looking union men strolling back and forth between the front door of the baths and some trailers parked across the way.

"A movie," one of the students replied. "With Alan Bates and Bette Midler."

Good god. *The Rose*. Word had been out for some months that Bette Midler was making her big-time movie debut (at last) in a film based on the career of Janis Joplin, and a lot of people weren't too happy about it, including the late rock singer's parents, who had given their permission instead to a project scripted by Myra Friedman, based on her sensitive biography of Joplin, *Buried Alive*. The Midler project was generally feared to be a rip-off of the whole Joplin legend, right down to its title (allegedly a reference to the rose tattoo Janis had acquired on a trip to Brazil).

But, lo and behold, Janis Joplin had never performed in a bathhouse, whereas Midler herself had begun her whole climb to fame and fortune by singing for gay men in towels (or less) at the infamous Continental Baths on New York's Upper West Side. Maybe *The Rose* wasn't going to be such a Joplin rip-off after all; maybe there was as much Midler in it as there was Joplin. Maybe Midler's own protestations to the press were true —that it wasn't *really* about Janis at all, but about "all those women," from the blues singers to the sixties rockers, the ones who sang and suffered, suffered and sang, and didn't quite survive.

The superstar mystique had always been important to Midler—she had fantasized about it, nurtured herself on it, made it her own. In the mid-seventies she became what any self-respecting would-be superstar had to be—a pop-music idol —though she certainly got to the top in her own very original and idiosyncratic way.

But now it was time to go after the real stardom, the kind that would be much more lasting than anything preserved in mere vinyl or platinum: celluloid immortality, the goddessdom of the Technicolor, Dolby-Sound-System-ed Silver Screen. The movies.

More than any other culture, America has worshiped its movie queens, those larger-than-life heroines who somehow made up for the fact that there were no male hero-figures on the scene, either in real life (where the few who showed any potential were gunned down by assassins' bullets) or on the screen. Growing up in the fifties, kids had to make do with cardboard cowboys or humorless private eyes. James Dean, Marlon Brando, and Montgomery Clift were kinky, rebellious, certainly interesting as actors. But not heroes, not leaders, and nowhere near as strong as a spunky Katharine Hepburn, a ballsy Bette Davis, or Joan Crawford bulldozing her way across the screen in her famous (and very inappropriately nicknamed) fuck-me pumps. America insisted, furthermore, that these superwomen (usually actresses or singers, or both) live up to these extraordinary self-imposed (or studio-imposed) myths, and in some cases the cost was too great. Garbo fled, but at least survived. Others did not: Monroe, Garland, Bessie Smith, Billie Holiday. Joplin herself. It took a pretty brassy babe to hold up under the demands of the diva mystique, and not all of them made it.

Bette Midler grew up an unhappy kid, the victim of religious prejudice, self-doubts about her personal appearance, and what seems to have been a rather peculiar family situation. Like many little average Americans, she escaped to television and radio, movies and rock 'n' roll. Divaland. She decided—early—that she was going to be a star, and became one.

The road was a rough one. Most of us have come to believe that the American Dream is a myth at best, that it's dangerous to fill kids' heads with all that Abraham Lincoln–Horatio Alger crap. A year or so ago, one might have said that Bette Midler was trying to become something that didn't exist—a movie magazine dream, a publicity-stunt come-on with no actual basis in reality.

Except that she did it. She went after superstardom and got it. She won, and she's now in the position to do whatever she wants with her success, even shuck the whole thing, which some observers consider a distinct possibility.

But whatever happens to Bette Midler now —whether she goes on to become a really significant record stylist, a dramatic actress on the stage or screen, or just a funky little housewife—doesn't really matter. Her significance has already been. The damage is done. Bette Midler and her alter ego, the Divine Miss M, made it from the Tubs (her phrase for a popular gay steambath in New York City) to the Top.

Maybe it's not such a bad thing, because in becoming a superstar, Midler didn't become a stereotype. She liberated—exploded—the image instead. She took the fantasy trip and brought it down to earth. She trashed it, by giving the folks not their traditional idea of glamour, but *her* idea —"trash with flash, sleaze with ease," as she is fond of calling it onstage. All of a sudden people started *enjoying* themselves in the theater again, and found themselves a new star to boot—this outrageous, wonderful, completely nutty *homely* woman who, heavens forfend, got her start by appealing to a gay vanguard every bit as spunky and outrageous as herself.

And with a firm grip on that reality, she's been able to give us all sorts of fantasy and fun in the bargain. And to help other performers, other solo entertainers, realize that by getting into themselves, into exploring honestly what it is that they actually have to offer as artists and communicators, they too can come up with something worthwhile. And maybe even become stars. Divas.

But to really grasp the impact that Bette Midler has had on contemporary culture and entertainment, one must first understand the Midler experience at its greatest height thus far, before repetition and boredom and confusion about where to go and what to do next set in and soured everything. To do this, we must go back to her finest performances to date—her Tony-Award-winning engagement at the legendary Palace Theater in New York in December of 1973.

1. The end of the beginning

from the pits to the palace

Three young ladies appear, wearing pink waitress outfits, complete with ruffly white aprons, and singing the Emerald City "Optimistic Voices" song from *The Wizard of Oz*. The audience barely has time to adjust to that when the lyrics proceed to "Open—aaah!—open—ah!" and the curtains do indeed part, revealing not Dorothy's ruby slipper but a giant silver-lamé platform-heel shoe that fills the whole stage of New York's Palace Theater. Down it walks Bette Midler, red hair raging, short frame slinking inside a sequined gown that iridesces its way back and forth between pink and lavender, her shoulders draped with a green, blue, orange, and yellow boa, singing "Lullaby of Broadway."

You could see her tongue in her cheek all the

way from the balcony. Bette Midler was making her big-time Broadway starring debut, so she was doing it up royally with a production number to end all production numbers, because it was a put-on of production-numbers-to-end-all-production numbers. But with just the right amount of zing to the satire so that the people who really like that sort of thing wouldn't be offended. Or not *too* offended. Especially since Bette Midler's not all that removed from liking that sort of thing a bit herself.

The secret of Midler's spectacular success is, in fact, exactly that—her approach to material. She approaches any song that she picks—from any source, period, or style—with a curious mixture of respect and daring. And whether she opts for nearly exact duplication of the original (as with the Andrews Sisters' "Boogie Woogie Bugle Boy") or an experimental stylistic statement of her own (as with Bob Dylan's "I Shall Be Released"), she has *fun* with her material: she finds life and humor and pathos in it, and she delivers what she finds to her audience.

Midler also views entertainment itself, the very act of performing, as material—as subject matter that she can not only use but comment on. She can do a put-on production number because she understands what a *good* production number is, because the comment is the audience-pleasing equivalent of the real thing.

Her own act is freewheeling and madcap, often giving the impression of complete inprovisation, which it isn't at all. Midler's one of the most careful planners in the business, but she's interested in freedom of performance style. She therefore works within a framework that's always loose enough to retain the *look* of freedom on the stage but structured enough to carry her consistently through a three-month tour and a three-week engagement at the Palace.

Bette's ticket sales for the New York engagement made Broadway history, setting a new record for biggest one-day advance sale ever for any theater on the Great White Way. Her thirty-five-city national tour prior to the Palace engagement is reported to have grossed three million dollars. Bette Midler had come a long way from a minor role in *Fiddler on the Roof* and singing after the show for free at two small clubs called Hilly's and the Improvisation. And a long way from singing for gay men in towels at the Continental Baths in the days before news of her own success helped turn that steamy showcase into a gaudy giggle for the New York jet set.

Prior to the Palace, Bette's face had hit the covers of *Cash Box, Record World, Rolling Stone, After Dark, Ms. Magazine, Modern Hi-Fi and Stereo Guide,* and the *New York Sunday News Magazine.* (The Palace brought her *Newsweek* as well.) A year before, *Record World* had dubbed her "This Year's Musical Superstar" and a "sensation," an opinion shared by veteran rock writer Robert Christgau, *Cash Box,* and (can you stand it?) Rona Barrett, who called her "today's answer to Texas Guinan and Mae West." In March of 1973, *The National Observer* gave her lead feature section coverage as "probably the brightest, hottest superstar to rise above the pop-music horizon in the 70s."

After the Palace engagement, Ruth Gordon and Garson Kanin both told columnist Ed Sullivan that Bette was among their top five "all time femme great" performers, an honor she shared with such pros as Katharine Hepburn, Jeanne Eagels, Laurette Taylor, and Hazel Dawn. Rex Reed called her "a legend in the making." And Earl Blackwell, the designer, who had accompanied actress Ruth Ford to the Palace opening, named Miss Midler to top his "Ten Worst Dressed Women" list, defining her style as "potluck in a laundromat."

Not that Miss M felt much more kindly toward the Earl Blackwell crowd who came to her debut. "You should have seen them," she told the audiences on succeeding nights at the Palace. "It was all Pucci and Gucci. Oh, my dear, it was the night of the living dead."

Outside, United Scenic Artists Local 829 members were picketing the big show, passing out leaflets saying that the designs were below their standards, and in the lobby, some of Miss M's older—and somewhat less stalwart—fans were horrified to find that a painting of Judy Garland had been taken down and one of the reigning box-office diva put up instead (Judy's picture was back in its old spot in the Palace lobby a few days later, which just goes to show that lobbying isn't dead, even on Broadway). The theater manager later confided, "The whole audience was nuts as far as I'm concerned," in reply to a question as to whether or not he recalled any juicy anecdotes about the engagement.

But onstage was where the action really was, and up there, walking the same boards that such theater greats as Sarah Bernhardt, Fanny Brice, Mae West, Sophie Tucker, George Burns and Gracie Allen had trod decades before her, was Bette Midler.

After a hula-dancer prologue (dues to the roots —Miss Midler hails from Honolulu) and a bit of Ikettes-like warming-up by Bette's own back-up ladies, the Harlettes, Miss M herself comes on strong in white pants, loud Hawaiian shirt and lei, singing her standard opener, "Friends." Her face contorts through the slow-opening bars, then she laughs and claps her way into the upbeat section, stepping to the edge of the stage and shaking hands with the people in the front row, then step-ping back, her hands still flying, slashing space like a conductor without a baton. Her eyes are open wide. She puts her hands on her hips, starts lifting her knees high in the air, as if the bulky platform shoes she's wearing weighed nothing at all. She takes small steps, though, much the way Janis Joplin did, but the footwork carries her quickly all over the stage, back and forth, up and down. Her arms and wrists move constantly, al-ways in exceptional co-ordination. Her whole body looks alive and alert, and it's obvious that I hadn't seen her at dance concerts regularly for mere amusement. She was *working*.

With the first song over, she dishes the "Puccis

and Guccis" from opening night, going on to add, "You should have smelled it. Nouveau leather everywhere. And all those people with real tight cheeks and small mouths. Oh, I tell you, *we were not pleased!*

"We're gonna do everything we know," she continues. "Here are three numbers I don't know at all," she says, indicating the Harlettes, "three ex-chorus girls from *Rachael Lily Rosenbloom*." (A little in-joke about a Broadway musical that had closed during previews a few days before without even opening. In it the main character was clearly patterned after Bette; she turned down a reported half-million dollars to play the role herself and it was then taken by Ellen Greene.)

Next comes another dig: "I'd now like to do one of Miss Reddy's greatest hits," Bette says, introducing "Delta Dawn," which both she and Helen Reddy had recorded. Her voice rasps and breaks at several points during the song; the strain of four months on the road is obvious. Still, the outline of the song remains intact, and even with some missed notes it retains most of its impact. She points her index finger up into the air on the last note, and then proceeds to miss it anyway, but the audience still demands an encore, which the Harlettes handle, for the most part, by themselves.

Switching to current events, she begins: "Rockefeller quit. Well, whataya know?" (The Governor of New York had indeed announced his resignation that day.) "This is just too much polit-ical news for me. The doors just keep *opening* and *closing*. It's like ships deserting a sinking rat, that's what it is. And *Rose Mary Woods!* That was the best. You don't think Nixon's sockin' it to her, do you? He's not sockin' it to anybody. He only socked it to Pat twice and he didn't do too good a job then. Did I really say that?"

Then, without pause: "This is the grossest song we do. I know you're all sitting there saying, 'Gross me out, gross me out.' You're cheap. This song is a good education for most people." She launches into a few bars of Seth Allen's "Bad Sex" (from the Off-Off-Broadway show, *Sissy*, directed by John Vaccaro for his Play-House of the Ridiculous).

"Actually there's no such thing," she says following "Bad Sex." "There are only people who don't fit together, that's all." (Some applause.) "This next song was sung by the late, great Miss Bessie Smith." (Very little applause.) "Oh, Bessie will be so *pleased!* Anyway, this song is the other side of the coin." And she belts out Bessie's good-sex song, "Empty Bed Blues," always one of Bette's most successful numbers.

The Harlettes sit down in big fan-shaped bamboo chairs, and Bette goes on to good-naturedly insult the "Looney Tunes in the front row tonight," and to admit, "Sarah Bernhardt is probably turning over in her grave. Get that bitch out of there, she's saying. She's nothing but a foul-mouthed vulgarian." Then she hoped that it wasn't "the Quaalude crowd up in the balcony—if so, please hang on to your chairs. The people in the orchestra just hate it when you fall over."

Before "Hubba Hubba," she talks about "The

'40s, I wasn't there, but I hear it had everything, wars, revolutions, floods, and plagues. What we're going to do tonight is put the vocal with the instrumental. Oh, *fab-u-lous*, a new taste sensation . . . There's a great horn section in this. And those three young ladies over there. Talk about horns. They're just the horniest . . ."

Next rap (after "In the Mood," during which she and the girls remain seated) is about the shows which have played the Palace, including one which "had a vegetable ballet—oh, very festive—and a fruit ballet. Imagine rutabagas walking up and down the aisles. It was really extravagant."

She starts to introduce her "bar song," interrupts herself when she thinks she sees Jerome Robbins (he directed her in *Fiddler*) in the audience, then goes on: "I like bars. Wayne Newton on the jukebox. You know they don't get any sleazier than that." Then "Drinking Again." Nice.

"We don't usually do this next song," she confides. "We had to eighty-six it because it's one of Karen Carpenter's greatest hits." (Laughter.) "No, now, I'm sure she's a great singer, but her drumming really sucks. She's clean, the cleanest thing I ever did see. Actually she and Tricia Nixon are at a tie. I don't want to dish *her*, though. She's gone through enough pain as it is. I'd be all embarrassed if that was *my* old man." Her delivery of "Superstar" is slow-driving, syncopated, full of beautifully controlled energy. She looks very vulnerable in the soft spotlight, and the words come across with exceptional meaning. A much deserved standing ovation which elicits, "Girls, I'm so happy, my cup runneth over, c'mon, girls, let's shake tits for these people." (Never lets us get too serious, this lady.)

In introducing her Philadelphia medley, Bette pauses with, "Wait. I have to do my Betsy Ross number. I went to Valley Forge and lit a candle for Miss Ross, whose real name was Rothschild. This is my impression of Betsy Ross, a sweet *yenta* holding up her flag: 'Do you think it's too busy?'

"Why does she bother," Bette interrupts herself, "why doesn't she just sing?"

She sits down on a stool, tells the audience she's pooped and that after the next song, "I Shall Be Released," she's going to give them a few minutes "to get really wasted, however you like." But first, "You gotta give people their two-dollar-and-fifty-cent show," followed by a double-take to the front row and, "You mean you paid twelve dollars to come here? That's the truth? You could have bought three gallons of gasoline for that kind of money!" She even jokes about her own ticket prices.

"Released" is driving, powerful, very Joe Cocker in its delivery. Bette's hands, legs, forearms, fingers, everything are going wildly, rhythmically. Her hair shakes, her fists clench, her arms flop up, puppet-like, from the elbows, and the legs likewise are jerked up from the knees.

Intermission. A few songs by Barry Manilow. *The Wizard of Oz* meets the Howard Johnson waitresses. And then the shoe. "Boogie Woogie Bugle Boy," and during the standing ovation, the

Harlettes rip open their tacky pink uniforms to reveal American flag linings. "Oh, my God, this group is so cheap. C'mon girls, listen up, the span of their attention is very short, we've got to sock it to them." Meaning us.

"Do You Want to Dance?" gets introduced with, "Remember we are all greasers in the sight of God." A Sonja Henie impression ("Some of you are not interested in movies and furry hats like me").

A description of the tour: "We started out *many* years ago. At least fourteen months now. A tour Martha Raye would have given her eyeteeth for, except she doesn't have any any more. No, seriously, we toured two hundred and fifty cities in eleven minutes by Sherman tank and gas mask."

The Nixon-Linda Lovelace joke ("Nixon saw *Deep Throat* ten or twelve times trying to get it down Pat"), Bette's German piece ("Oh, you're cheaper than I thought you were, 'I'd just love a German piece'"), "Surabaya Johnny," her American piece, "Hello in There."

In "Higher and Higher," the girls and their leader all get down to their slips (the four satiny garments being emblazoned with card suits—a heart, a club, a spade, and a diamond). Lots of knees and hips.

Introductions: "Each one of these girls has her name listed in the Manhattan telephone directory and they'd be very glad to hear from you." Robin is "so clean you could eat off her and she wouldn't mind." Sharon was picked up "at Disneyland where she was working as one of the rides." Charlotte, in the slip with a spade, does a filthy bump 'n' grind that blots out all memory of her introduction/insult. The band is in street clothes; the back-up brass section in tuxes.

"She's finally going to do it," Bette speaks again for the crowd. "It only took her two hours, the bitch." She turns her backside. "It's a fabulous ass, ain't it?" Does the splits and falls on the floor. "Now you're saying: That's the first thrill I've had since she began. My God, she's breaking her neck." A big valentine descends for "Chapel of Love." Bette becomes choir leader to the whole audience, who are now all standing as the house lights come up.

A quick reprise of "Friends" and it's over.

2. roots and dues

from oahu to the improv

"I stood there looking up at that gigantic billboard of Bette over the Palace," recalls Gail Kantor, one of Midler's original trio of back-up singers, "and I had an image in my head of a schlumpy little girl that I knew standing there looking up and thinking back of everything she had to do to get there."

Bette Midler was born December 1, 1945, in Honolulu, Hawaii. Her parents were from Paterson, New Jersey. As Bette put it to Dick Leitsch of *Gay*, "they migrated early in life to Paradise."

Bruce Vilanch, a newspaperman and funnyman who later became one of Bette's comedy writers, is from Paterson, too. "I remember the first time I saw her on the Carson Show," he says. "I was watching it with my parents. And they were looking and looking at the screen and all of the sudden my father said, 'That girl looks just like Ruth Goldberg. Who is that girl? Betty Midler? Didn't Ruth Goldberg marry a Midler? Chesty Midler, that's who she married. And they moved to Hawaii.' "

Chesty, whose real name was Fred, got his nickname, according to Vilanch, because of his "fabulous physique. He was the one son in a family of five girls, and the mother was incredibly possessive. Very, very protective, and he became very introverted and had few friends. He spent all of his time at the Y lifting weights." He ran away and joined the Navy eventually, and was stationed in Hawaii, which he quickly learned to like a lot more than New Jersey.

He returned home to Paterson and married Ruth Goldberg, whom Vilanch's father had once dated and who "was pretty well known in Paterson and came from a nice family." Though most of the rest of the Midlers in Paterson were in the dry-cleaning business, Chesty became a house painter and soon took his new wife with him back to Hawaii. They moved back to New Jersey once "for about six months, but it didn't work out," according to Vilanch. Then back to Hawaii, for good.

Bette was one of four children. Her sister, Judith, was killed when hit by a car while visiting Bette in New York during Bette's stint in *Fiddler on the Roof*. She has an older sister, Susie, who now sublets Bette's New York apartment, and a younger brother, Danny. Bette's mother (who

named her for Bette Davis) shared her daughter's
fascination for the theater and movies (she's the
type who "saves clippings and everything," Bette
told an interviewer from the *National Observer*).
Mrs. Midler died of cancer in early 1979. Her
father, by all reports, remained a very quiet, introverted man. Vilanch calls him "a very strange,
strange fellow. He became very conservative in
Hawaii. They've always lived surrounded by Sa-
moans and Filipinos and everything, and his best
friends are all Hawaiians, but he's a raging
conservative."

Bette herself told Neil Appelbaum of *After
Dark*: "My mother and father were very eccentric.
I adored them. My father liked machinery so
there were five cars in the backyard, three refrig-
erators and six washing machines in the kitchen,
and the living room had a buzz saw. Nothing
worked. Unbelievable. Living in that house was
heavy."

The program notes for the Palace state: "She
grew up in Hawaii, the only Jewish girl in a work-
ing-class Samoan neighborhood. Her vivid memories of childhood include avoiding street fights
with her tougher classmates and spending hours
in movie theaters. 'I used to wander the old red
light district,' she says, 'the tacky part of town.
And it looked very romantic and passionate to
me, so alive. See, even then I was always fascinated by the bad girls. It seemed like the bad girls
always had the most fun.'"

Though Bette was born in Honolulu, the family
moved to nearby Aiea, which she described to Jan

Bette at the Bitter End, May, 1972. (Photos by Robert Morris)

Bette at home on Barrow Street in New York's Greenwich Village. (Photos by Robert Morris)

Hodenfeld of *The New York Post* as, "a rural community between sugarcane fields and across from the fleet-training city." (She dubbed it "a slum right near Pearl Harbor," in talking to *Newsweek*.) It was a tough neighborhood. (She compared it to Harlem for Hodenfeld, and said that the Filipinos were the toughest in the neighborhood, with the Portuguese running a close second: "I wasn't Portuguese, but I let them think it because it was easier than anything else. Portuguese people were accepted. Jews were not.")

Bette told May Okun of the New York *Daily News*: "We lived in a fabulous place called Halauua Housing—poor people's housing. At the time, I really hated it—I was an alien, a foreigner, even though I was born there—but now I have very fond memories of it."

The only Jewish girl in her grade school, she was (as she told a writer for *Modern Hi-Fi*), "always getting unexcused absences for Jewish holidays." In the first grade (according to *Cash Box*) she "won the prize" for singing "Silent Night" —"It was fun, but I felt guilty because I was Jewish and I wasn't supposed to be singing Christmas carols."

The school years were not happy ones. "I was miserable as a child," she told Appelbaum. "I guess it was because I looked like I do. Media have told us we're supposed to look a certain way. They really do a job on you. I used to try to dress like other people but I never could go there. I was never together. That wasn't my way. It would have been one thing if I had been a beautiful child, but I was a plain little fat Jewish kid." The other girls, in particular, made things unpleasant for her at school, as she told Ed McCormack of *Rolling Stone*, "because I had big boobs. At the tender age of fourteen or fifteen, they were quite phenomenal."

Growing up, she told Hodenfeld, was "very exotic and very American at the same time. You would get 'American Bandstand' and *Screen Gems* magazine, and then you would have your Chinese greasers and your Japanese bike girls, and it was very strange."

Bette made some rather telling statements about her early home life to New York *Daily News* writer Stan Mieses in 1977. "I'd like to be in control of my emotions," she said, "rather than let them be in control of me. In my house, everyone let go. No mysteries. If you're high-spirited and emotional, you find yourself in hot water most of the time. It's the hardest part of maturing."

Bill Hennessy, who probably got to know Bette better than anyone during the first years of her career (he met her while doing her hair during *Fiddler* and later became her comedy writer, close confidant and traveling companion during the early tour dates), says: "A lot of her force, a lot of her feelings came from all of those things, from watching movies, a great deal from watching movies, plus a lot of it from the '50s, from growing up in Hawaii. And that whole feeling of 'American Bandstand.'

"It's very complex," Hennessy continues, "because Bette was a highly academic girl. She was quite intelligent in school. If you've seen early pictures, she had on little glasses. There was no going to the bars and being a tough lady, but there was a tough lady inside. No, 'tough lady,' that's a bad term. A free human being that was inside her, waiting to get out, and it came out later when she created The Divine Miss M. All those fantasies that she had just came out, and she did them all onstage. So, whatever fantasy she had, whether it was Nancy Walker or the Shangri-La's, all of that is a conglomeration of her fantasies."

Bette told McCormack: "I guess I was very inward when I was young. You wouldn't believe it, but I was very shy, stayed by myself and read a lot, lived very much in my head, in my daydreams."

Most of those daydreams were about the theater or the movies. "By the time I was in my senior year in high school," she said to McCormack, "I was completely stage-struck and had made up my mind that eventually I would come to New York."

Effecting that decision was not quite as easy as making it. First came a year at the University of Hawaii and a summer job in a pineapple cannery. She had moved out of the house because she was involved with a man and (as she told May Okun), "didn't want my ma to know."

The souvenir program from *Fiddler on the Roof* says she was "a surf bunny in a Bikini beach movie, *Surf-a-go-go*," which may or may not be a put-on. She did play a missionary's wife ("All I did was heave over the edge of the ship," she's told several interviewers) in George Roy Hill's *Hawaii*. (Steven Paley, who was an apprentice film editor on the film, recalls that Hill was quite impressed with Midler and said that he was going to "keep my eye on her" for a role in the musical version of *The World of Henry Orient* which he was to direct on Broadway. Alice Playten eventually got the role instead.)

Hawaii was responsible for getting Bette to New York. As she explained to Miss Okun: "I was paid three-hundred dollars a week and seventy dollars per diem, and I lived on two dollars a day. When it was over, I took my money—my little savings pot with one thousand dollars—and I came to New York at the end of 1965. I left fifteen-hundred dollars at home, just in case I had to go back, or in case they had to send it to me . . . I wanted the money to last. I think I still have that original thousand dollars."

Bette arrived in New York City, as she once told television viewers on Johnny Carson's *Tonight Show*, with "a lot of anger in me built up from those years." And determined to be a star.

The early days were at least exciting. As soon as she got to town, New York City had its big electricity blackout. Bette's first living quarters were in the Broadway Central Hotel (a building which later collapsed), a favorite hang-out for derelicts and assorted weirdos ("I developed a lot of wind running from all manner of strange people," she told Chris Chase for a piece in *The New York Times*).

She took an assortment of jobs: typing and filing at Columbia University, selling gloves at Stern's Department Store, working as a go-go girl in Union City, New Jersey. Buddy Fox, later manager of the most popular of New York's cabarets, Reno Sweeney, hired Bette to work the checkroom of the Downtown discotheque (located at One Sheridan Square, in quarters later occupied by clubs called Salvation and When We Win, now both defunct) when a friend of hers, Pam Chilton, graduated to dancer. Bette eventually became a dancer, too (not go-go, but social; three guys and three girls were hired by the club to give the impression that "something was already happening" at the club each night, according to Fox), and suggested her roommate, Meredith Bodien (whom Fox later married) for the checkroom job.

Fox recalls: "My impression of her at that time was that she was very ambitious and a very hard worker. She was taking classes all around town, acting, singing, dancing, in fact, she and Meredith met at HB Studio, where they were both studying acting. I think even then" (this was the winter of 1966–67) "she was putting her act together, creating the Divine Miss M. Bette was just going to succeed. She had dramatic presence. Even then, she could be a comedienne, light or heavy, from Joanne Woodward to Lucille Ball."

Bette told May Okun that she "just blossomed out" on arriving in New York. "I never felt I was home 'til I came here. I became all the things I wanted to be. It was like I was finally free."

Shortly after arriving she called playwright and Off-Off-Broadway director Tom Eyen, saying that she was just in from Hawaii and had gotten his name from a girlfriend. At that time, he was casting *Miss Nefertiti Regrets* for a run at Ellen Stewart's Café La Mama, and Bette asked for an audition, although Eyen told her he thought he didn't really need any more people. She came by the next day and sang "Pirate Jenny" for him. Eyen gave her one of the non-speaking roles ("Just in the chorus, one of the schleppers," actor William Duff-Griffin recalls), but when the show was revived a few months later, Bette was cast in the title role of the sexy Egyptian queen (in blond wig, bikini, and stiletto heels).

Duff-Griffin acted in another Eyen play with Bette. "It was Tom's version of *Cinderella*, which we did at the 13th Street Theatre at about this time. We did a kid's version in the afternoon and an adult version at night, changing the 'C' in Cinderella to an 'S,' *Sin*derella, you know. It was very daring. We did things like drink highballs out of glass slippers. Then, in 1968, when she was in *Fiddler*, Bette did another children's show for Tom. It was called *Alice Through the Glass Lightly*, with music by Jonathan Kramer, from the original cast of *Hair*. Bette was the Red Queen and came out with a big red umbrella to sing 'What a Lovely Day to Play Croquet.'"

Eyen's shows, which are composed primarily of the kind of bitchy one-liners Bette herself was later to become known for onstage, were not the only Off-Off-Broadway theater Bette became acquainted with during this period. Her Palace program notes state: "About that time, Bette saw a production of the Theatre of the Ridiculous and was deeply impressed. 'There was this character, Waterfront Woman. I'll never forget her. I wanted to be just like her.'"

The reference was probably to Black-Eyed Susan, an actress now with Charles Ludlam's Ridiculous Theatrical Company (one of the two significant splinter groups from the original Theatre of the Ridiculous troupe; the other is John Vaccaro's Play-House of the Ridiculous), in Ludlam's *Turds in Hell*. Bette told Lisa Robinson for *Interview*: "I got a great deal of my early inspiration from Charles Ludlam. The first thing I ever saw him do was *Turds in Hell*, which blew me away. It was incredible, it was the most incredible piece of theater I had ever seen. And there was this chick in the show called Black-Eyed Susan—did you ever see her?—she was terrific, she really inspired me." She elaborated further to Cynthia Spector in *Zoo World*, "She was kind of a running-gag character. In one part she was a hooker on the docks, and she came out and recited this endless Robert Service poem that made no sense at all. Then in this 1930s number she came out all wrapped in toilet paper with dollar bills taped to her. She was the Statue of Liberty and sang 'Wheel of Fortune.'" She also told Spector: "That's what I get from the Theatre of the Ridiculous" (Spector didn't capitalize it, but the reference is clearly to the Ludlam-Vaccaro group), "the sardonic side of it. What good is it if you can't giggle at it, 'cos in the long run that's all it is."

Next came her three-year run in *Fiddler on the Roof* on Broadway, first as a member of the chorus, then as the older daughter, Tzeitel (where she got to sing "all of thirty-two bars," as she told *Newsweek*'s Robert Michener). "Tzeitel is a good role," she said to Dick Leitsch of *Gay*. "I loved it for two years, which is a long time for anybody to love it."

Marta Heflin understudied Bette in *Fiddler* and did the role when Bette's sister Judith was killed. "It was a terrible, terrible thing. I was there at her house for sitting *shiva*. I was very impressed with her then. Because it was a terrible tragedy. But she was very strong. You could tell that she was very upset, but she was very strong. She's a very strong lady, you know. You saw those guts coming through. I'll never forget that. There was no self-pity, no breast-beating. I did the role for a week-and-a-half, and then she was back."

Marta then moved on to a role in an Off-Broadway musical called *Salvation*. When she in turn left that show, she recommended Bette for the role, knowing that she was by that time itching to get out of playing Tzeitel eight times a week. "She was terrific in her audition," Marta said, "so she took over my part. She did the same songs, totally different."

Salvation was Bette's last go-around with musical theater to date, except for a brief run in *Tommy* (playing the double role of Mrs. Walker and the Acid Queen) with the Seattle Opera Company in May 1971. Another whole thing was already beginning to happen, which was to bring Bette back to Broadway in triumph, but via a very different route.

While understudying Bette in *Fiddler*, Marta Heflin, on the advice of her vocal coach, had started singing for free at some late-night theater-crowd clubs around town. When Bette got wind of what she was doing, she asked Marta if she could come along.

Her singing debut was at Hilly's, a small club located down on 9th Street in Greenwich Village. She described the experience for Lisa Robinson in *Interview* as follows:

"The first two songs were okay—they weren't anything special, but the third song—something just happened to my head and my body and it was just the most wonderful sensation I'd been through. It wasn't like me singing, it was something else.

"The song was 'God Bless the Child,' which I don't sing, I never sing it. I sang it once and that was all, because it frightened me so, it really freaked me out. I was screaming at the end of it, the song had a life of its own and the song imposed itself on me and I didn't even know what was going on. I was just the instrument for what was going on."

Bette and Marta started going regularly to

Hilly's, and to another club, called the Improvisation, on West 44th Street.

"Hilly's had a little stage and it was very intimate," Marta recalls. "It was very folksy, very Villagey. Kind of dark and musty. Smoky. And the owners were very un-show-bizy, you know. It was nice, very relaxed, much like what I imagine the old jazz clubs were like. I enjoyed singing there more. The Improv was nerve-wracking to me. I really looked forward to going out and singing after the show every night, though. It was like —*sin*—you know. It was like transgressing from what I thought I really wanted to do, until it began to *be* what I really wanted to do."

Bette got increasingly excited about their newfound avocation as well. "I remember in the dressing room when I was up there," Marta says. "Bette used to say things like, 'I've got this great idea. I'm going to get together all these old songs and do them. That's what I'm going to do.' She was really hepped up about it. It was almost like a direction for her to go after that tragedy with her sister. It was like, I'm going to sink my teeth into life. And get every bit of this out. It was really something to see."

Partly through her boyfriend, a dancer from *Fiddler* named Ben Gillespie, Bette began to get particularly excited about the old-time torch singers, like Helen Morgan. Sheila Weller, in an article in *Modern Hi-Fi and Stereo Review*, quotes her as saying that she went out to a junk shop and bought a black velvet gown with beaded sleeves after seeing a picture of Helen Morgan on an album cover: "Ten dollars, and it's still the most beautiful thing in my closet."

Ben also introduced Bette to the talents of Aretha Franklin, an event which she has described as a major turning point in her music-listening career, particularly hearing Aretha's tribute album to Dinah Washington, *Unforgettable*. When I spoke to her in October 1970 for an article for *The Chicago Daily News*, Bette termed the album ". . . a real awakening. It was like I had no idea what music was all about until I heard her sing. It opened up the whole world."

The world it opened was one that Bette immediately began to research. She started buying and listening to records carefully, and would even spend her days off (when there was not a *Fiddler* matinee) at the Lincoln Center Library for the Performing Arts, looking up old songs. Budd Friedman, the owner of the Improvisation and the man who became Bette's first manager, describes her at this period as one of the hardest workers he's ever known: "She'd go out and dig up songs, would talk to people and dig brains. She was always out looking for new material. Nobody does that any more." Or, at least, practically nobody was doing it in 1970.

Unlike Hilly's, the Improvisation *was* show biz. Budd Friedman planned it that way. After a brief career in advertising, Friedman decided in 1962 to open a "coffeehouse with food" (as the Improv was for a while, prior to getting a liquor license) when he and his girlfriend (an actress named Silver Saundors who was then appearing in *Fiorello*) noticed that there was no place around where young people in the theater could go after shows and be able to get up and perform in a showcase situation.

The Improv became known primarily as a stand-up comic's room (David Steinberg, David Frye, Richard Pryor, Jimmy Walker, Freddie Prinze, and Dick Cavett did some of their first performing there), but young singers were also on the bill (besides Bette and Marta, Alaina Reed, Daphne Davis, Liz Torres, and even Liza Minnelli did some of their early experimenting in the room).

Friedman doesn't recall being particularly impressed when Bette first sang at the club. "She came in and sang a couple of dirges, as she put it, or as we mutually put it. You know, *Threepenny Opera* shit." A few months later he went to another club called the African Room to hear a singer named Roz Harris, whom he was considering managing. Bette was also on the bill, and Friedman heard her do "Am I Blue" for the first time. "I forgot all about the other idea and said to Bette immediately, 'Gee, you've got to come to the Improv again.' She did, and after about a month I decided to manage her."

Friedman says that the reception to Bette was good "most of the time, but once in a while there were some people who just didn't understand what she was doing. I remember once a crowd started laughing at her, just because of the way she looked as she walked up the aisle. But by the time she finished her first song, they were no longer laughing. It was perhaps the bizarreness of it that they didn't understand. She was bizarre even then. But I always had the greatest faith in her. I knew she was going to be a star. I kept telling people, 'That girl's gonna be a star.' "

During the year that he managed Bette's career, Friedman pulled several major coups, getting her on television's *The David Frost Show*, *The Merv Griffin Show* and *The Tonight Show* (host Johnny Carson of the last particularly took to Bette and invited her back regularly), as well as her first paying club dates: Paul's Mall in Boston, Mister Kelly's in Chicago, and the biggest surprise of all —an engagement that was to establish her image and her career—sixteen weeks at the Continental Baths, a popular sex-and-sauna spa for homosexuals on Manhattan's Upper West Side.

3. the emergence of miss m

from the baths to the bitter end

It was mid-1970. Bette Midler picked up the phone. Bill Hennessy, who had been the company hairdresser when she was in *Fiddler*, was on the other end of the wire.

"Bette?" he began. "You're not going to believe this, but I was just over at the Continental Baths and there was this sign on the wall. There's some drag queen who's calling himself Bette Midler and plans to appear there this weekend."

In one fell swoop, Bette had a joke to use to break the ice opening night at the Baths—and Bill Hennessy was on the verge of leaving his curling irons behind for a career in singer management.

The working relationship clicked immediately, and it is generally acknowledged that Bill was extremely instrumental in the creation of the Divine Miss M, the stage persona that had so much to do with skyrocketing Bette Midler to superstardom.

Miss M is complex, contradictory, full of little inconsistencies and surprises—almost as much so as Bette herself. The character runs the gamut from camp to pathos, has a double image of brassy bitch and vulnerable child-woman. She is Joplin—and Sophie Tucker. Helen Morgan and Mae West. Some memories of Bessie Smith and Billie Holiday. A touch—and *just* a touch—of Streisand and Garland. Bits and pieces of a whole tradition. Plus Bette Midler. A lot of Bette Midler.

Photographer Peter Dallas, an early friend of Bette, probably summed up the Miss M mystique as succinctly as anyone: "What Bette created onstage was essentially her *self*, seen *through the eyes* of Bill Hennessy."

Bill had been watching lady singers and comics for years—and would go home and re-do their acts, in his own mind and on paper. Writing new lines for them. Telling them (in his own imagination) what worked and what didn't. Occasionally, he'd try out a joke or two on some of the women at the Improv. But his real chance to create came with Bette at the Baths.

"It got to the point where I would not just write lines," he says, "but I'd tell her other things as well, how to come onstage, how to deliver the material. Never how to sing, but almost everything else.

"Her instincts were incredible. What she did was to sort of mime me, to a great extent. Copy what I'd be doing. It was almost like exchanging my personality for hers. It was a very complex thing. I was writing, I was choreographing the movements, I was directing, almost as if I were up there doing it, but always with her insight and her perception in mind. Her talent.

"Bette has always admired me as being a very funny person. She liked who I was, and she took whatever she could from me."

Bette usually refers to the Continental affectionately as the Tubs. Actually there were no tubs. Just some showers, a sauna and a steamroom, a sun deck on the roof, and a big swimming pool.

But, as with most Turkish bathhouses which cater to homosexuals (and the now defunct Continental made no secret about its clientele), the real action is elsewhere. In the "private rooms" (small cubicles just large enough for a cot-sized bed and a tiny bedside table), or in one big room upstairs, called "the dormitory," but more affectionately (and accurately) known as "the orgy room."

Gay baths are nothing new to the New York scene and are now pretty common around the rest of the country as well (where they're usually private membership clubs). They are not merely places for a sexual pick-up, like a gay bar, but for sex itself. The customers roam the corridors in towels, waiting for what Alaina Reed refers to (in another context) as "the all-important nod" or peeping past the open doors of the private rooms. Or, they simply throw pretense to the wind and head up to the dormitory. Which is always dark, and crowded.

Gay people pay (often a great deal) for the privacy to do their thing at the Baths, and they are left alone, at least in New York. There are no hassles with the police, no raids, no names in the *Daily News.* Gay politicos insist, evidently with some justification, that the hands-off attitude has something to do with the links that the various New York baths are alleged to have with the city's two reigning mob families (an accusation often made about many of New York's gay bars as well).

Steve Ostrow, who ran the Continental, is a pompous and self-important man (the kind who would go on a morning television talk show with his wife and male lover to declare *himself* chicly bisexual), but at least he had the good business sense to open a gay bathhouse that was less seedy than most. Where liberated sex could flourish along with a certan amount of self-respect, minus the cockroaches. He took the quarters of the old Ansonia Hotel and gave New Yorkers a baths that was not only clean, but that even had facilities (toilets, sauna, steamroom) that worked.

Like many a well-run capital venture that fills a void, Ostrow's baths was an instant success. The ambience changed from cleanliness and self-respect to polish and "sophistication," then to interior-decorator self-conscious chic. There were soon a boutique selling Continental Baths towels, a bar with color television monitor showing first-run movies, red pool tables, and mirrors everywhere. Also the ear-piercing blast of discotheque speed-rock, that unworthy stepchild of the vital rhythm-and-blues of just a few years back, in the days when the Continental likewise wasn't into color-coordinated platform heels and visiting jet-setters out on their decadence/slumming trip. Different rhythms altogether.

Ostrow instituted entertainment (and supposedly his other "improvements") because, as he puts it: "I never wanted this particular place to stand for only one thing, sex. I never have. That's part of it, but that's part of life. This is a very full, living cycle, a total environment. It encompasses entertainment, politics, relationships, and even religion—the social, sexual, ethical, ethereal, spiritual, physical, athletic living situation. And after you've been here for twenty-four hours, or whatever, you want to be entertained. I do. Entertainment was part of my total environment, my living situation, so it was a natural thing to make a part of the Baths."

Ostrow's first act at the Baths was a husband-and-wife duo, Lowell and Rosalie Mark. Lowell wrote most of the material and accompanied his wife on acoustic guitar. The set-up was simple. As Ostrow describes it, "We brought her down and put her on a soapbox in the lounge. And hooked up a microphone and let it happen."

Rosalie, who later sang on the cabaret circuit again herself, remembers those first shows as, "Very quiet. Peaceful. It was totally different then than it is now. It was completely a concert situation. Genuine, honest, beautiful, warm, sincere.

The men were more peaceful. No one walked around nude. They wore towels and were very discreet. It was a different clientele. You had more of the creator, more of the doctor, more of the lawyer, more of the philosopher. It was a completely different place than it is today. There was no fear. There was no flurry, no spangles, no stars. It was warm."

The Marks played one night per week there for three months. Ostrow's next act was Bette, who had been mentioned to him by Bob Elston, a music and drama teacher at HB Studio. On Elston's recommendation Ostrow went to hear Bette at the Improv; he liked her and started her out singing Fridays and Saturdays, for eight weeks (the Friday nights were later dropped). Bette was then asked back for eight more weeks and later made some one-night-only "returns" to the Baths after her career began to take off.

The physical layout of the lounge area was still quite simple when Bette started out. A friend recalls: "There was no restaurant, no dance floor. It just resembled a bathhouse that was temporarily turned into a fairly small performing area. There was a dressing room up on the side, up a few steps. It was all kind of dingy actually—nothing spectacular the way it is today. None of the flash it has now—none of the gorgeous chairs, none of the fabulous lighting, none of the chicness. There were no seats for the audience. Everyone just sat on the floor or stood."

Bette asked Billy Cunningham (later musical director of the Off-Broadway show, *Let My Peo-*

ple Come), whom she knew from the Improvisation, to accompany her on piano. The first weekend was not a smashing success.

"The dressing room was tiny and had a barber chair in it," Billy relates. "So I told her I'd be out at the Pepsi counter when she was ready to go on. They cleared the dance floor and set up the chairs and made the announcement. I went to the piano. There was a smattering of applause from the people around. I played this great tom-te-tom introduction, and she came out.

"To say they loved her would not be true, because they didn't. They didn't love her that first night. They liked her. And the second night they liked her less, because she sang all the same songs that she sang the first night. But we didn't know —we didn't realize it was the same people who kept going back every weekend. I distinctly remember someone walking up to me and saying, 'She sang all that junk last night. I heard all that about her hairdresser doing her hair with an eggbeater. She's a talented girl, but she should get some fresh material.' "

Another friend who was there those first few weeks recalls only twenty or thirty people in the first few audiences. But then it started to build. Ostrow says, "She was a frightened little girl at first. They related to her, they sympathized with her. But the talent thing started to grow. From a simple, sincere performer, she started to get into relating with the audience, and she could get bitchier and bitchier, which at that time was a very in thing to be. And it worked."

Before long, Ostrow realized he had the makings of a phenomenal success on his hands. "The timing was right, the world was right, the gay situation was right, the life syle was right. I don't know if it could happen again. Everybody was in the right place at the right time."

Bette's repertory built steadily at the Baths. "She got the chance to try out a lot of things," says Billy Cunningham. "We did 'Come Up and See Me Some Time,' that old Sophie Tucker thing, a lot. And 'Remember My Forgotten Man,' and 'Am I Blue.' She opened with 'Am I Blue' that first night in fact, which I thought was a terrible idea, it's such a down song. But, she did it and it worked.

"She'd also do 'Bill Bailey.' And a really nice version of 'Lady Madonna,' very slow. Then, 'Honky Tonk Woman,' very fast, very up. And she closed with 'The Continental.' We thought it would be a hoot to close with 'The Continental' starting the second week. The first week we closed with some screaming rock number that I'd never heard before, or since."

Bette and Billy often clashed over material, both having very strong opinions about music. Bette would bring in a stack of sheet music to rehearsal, and Billy would toss song after song on the floor, sometimes leaving her in tears. "She'd say, 'But I want to do those songs,'" Billy recalls. "And I'd say, 'Well, you're not going to do them with me.' I mean, honestly, one day she decided that she wanted to do 'Home on the Range' in a minor key. I don't mean to denigrate her talent, there's certainly no small amount of talent there. She just happens not to have any taste."

They would also argue over arrangements, particularly Bette's tendency not to "lock things in," as Billy puts it. "Once at a rehearsal, we did a song eight times, and she did it differently every time. Finally, I said, 'Bette, we're not doing this song any more. *Settle* on it.' And she said, 'Just one more time.' So we did it once more, and the ninth version was different *again.* And two days later when we did it at the Continental, it was still different. Completely."

Billy wanted things "the way they should be," he says. "Now, I don't object to unexpected change. If you die onstage, I can cover it beautifully. No one will ever know that they're laying you out in the back in a wooden coffin and carting you off to Frank Campbell's, because I would just fill the moment up with music and bring down the lights. And no curtain call, no encore." Dying onstage was okay—but not changing your act in the middle of a set. Although Billy does admit, "Her spontaneity was one of the things that the kids loved. She would change the order of songs all the time. She'd say, 'Let's not do that one, let's do this one instead.' Right in the middle of the show. And I would do it. I would hate it, but I would do it."

As much as he respected her as a stylist ("Bette had a real talent and a real knack for understanding exactly what it was that the writer of a song meant. Not only what the lyrics meant, but the

whole thing, the whole feeling behind the song")
Billy was constantly irritated at her for not being
more organized and consistent: "Where did she
go to find her music? I don't know—I think Good-
will shops. She brought me things written on everything but Saran-Wrap, I swear to you. You
could see where every pianist she had ever
worked with had made his own notations. Stacks
and stacks of key changes and notations. And you
had to mark all that out or mark over it so you
could write in your own, or write in her current
version of it."

It was not a musical marriage made in heaven.
Bette had added Joey Mitchell on drums early in
the run at the Baths, and it wasn't long before
Billy made a quiet exit and Bette replaced him
with Barry Manilow, who was to serve as her
pianist, musical director, arranger and collabora-
tor all the way to the Palace.

"When Bette was at the Improvisation," says
Bill Hennessy, "she had this image that she was
going to be Helen Morgan. She had this feeling of
being reincarnated. And Ben Gillespie influenced
her greatly to be a torch singer. God knows, Bette
was a heavy singer with a long dress and all, at
that time.

"Well, when she went to the Baths, I said, 'That
isn't going to work. You've got to allow the comedy, the joy in your life to show through. *Be
insane.* And she was already developing a little bit
of her insanity, because she had just seen Joplin
on the stage about six months, or three months

prior to that, and it made a tremendous impact on her. In fact, she sprained her ankle the next night in *Fiddler*, after seeing Joplin."

Bill wanted the insanity, the zaniness of her humor to come out both in her patter between songs and in her whole attitude and awareness of her image onstage. "She was a funny lady herself, but at that particular time, she didn't have the instinct to bring it out onstage. She could be funny, but it was never big. So what she was doing then was to just sing mostly."

She had done some patter at the Improv (certainly more than most of the singers at that time were doing, Budd Friedman says), but Bill feels she didn't really find her comic identity ("the way to do it") until the Baths. The knack to rap successfully to the audience was not something that she acquired overnight. Bill says: "She had a tendency, until she really learned to trust me, to talk on. The lines were very short that I gave her, and like a lot of performers who are just starting out she would just keep going. Some people talk about everything but the joke, or they deliver the joke, and just before they get to the punch line, they'll fly off on some other tangent. So, a lot of the talk was off the top of her head, extemporaneous, about her family life or something else that we hadn't gotten into." Later, Bette and Bill would talk about the material, and often the best of the extemporaneous rambling would be incorporated into the act. It was always a two-way street.

Bill and Bette became close friends as well. He would walk her from her apartment on 75th Street to the Baths, which was a few blocks west on 74th Street. "We used to schlepp to the Baths, with a shopping bag full of her shoes, and her clothes in a cleaning bag. Some nights she'd say, 'Let's go across 75th Street instead of 74th Street tonight, because if we do it that way, maybe it will be good luck and we'll have a really good show.' I had visions that she was going to be a giant star, but at the same time, there we were. Writing all the jokes down on a piece of brown paper and drinking a glass of bourbon or smoking a joint before we left. And now to think of the enormous success."

The Hennessy-Midler combination seems to have been one of those rare working relationships, where professional respect is balanced by a feeling of close personal affinity. Bill remained, by all accounts, the single closest person ("other than her boyfriends," he smiles) to her throughout the entire first phase of her career—until, in fact, the second major force in building Bette's stardom appeared on the scene: Aaron Russo, who made Bette a national name by arranging two spectacular coast-to-coast tours (the second ending at the Palace), and who (as one member of that entourage put it) "alienated more of her friends than Bette will ever know" by such acts as locking her dressing room door to everyone, including Bill Hennessy.

Brian van der Horst, then in the publicity department of Atlantic Records, told *Record World* in November, 1972 (at the time of the issue of Bette's first album), that she had appealed so strongly to the gay customers of the Continental because "the current bohemia always discovers these people first." And gay liberation was indeed coming into its own. May Okun of the *New York News Magazine* put it: " 'The boys' saw in her a rebellious, kindred spirit. Her big, belting voice, imitating, parodying, wallowing in the past but making it all sound new, her campy clothes, letting it all hang out, she made them forget their long-time devotion to the classic fag-hags: Garland, Davis, and Tallulah."

Bette herself has said (to *Interview*) that "the whole thing changed when I started working at the Baths, from a fairly negative, bluesy down trip to a sort of semi-up trip," and (to *Newsweek*): "The Tubs encouraged me to explore satire, and the audience there wouldn't settle for half-ass. If I'd kept my distance, they'd have lost interest because there were too many other things going on in the building that were more fun."

Though she later regretted the jet-set direction the Continental took (*The National Observer* interview reports her as saying "with regret" that the Continental "got picked up by all the chic people as *the* place to go"), she has always acknowledged her sixteen weeks there as an extremely formative period of her career.

Bruce Vilanch, who like Bill Hennessy before him, became close friends with Bette while writing comedy material for her, sums up the Baths experience as follows: "I think she drew upon a lot of the types she saw at the Tubs to create her character. But the interesting thing is that that character is more universal than anyone suspected. It appeals to all sorts, all types."

The world in general (to say nothing of the entertainment world) was ready for a little liberation, after the tight restrictions of the previous two decades, and Bette's appeal to gay men to be themselves and to be happy in that identity was merely a microcosm of the message that she was to offer to the world at large.

"My manager has me booked to stay in the men's Y," Bette told Johnny Carson and Late Night Televisionland in October 1970, describing the accommodation Budd Friedman had made for her during her first engagement at Mister Kelly's in Chicago. "I think they have a special floor for women," she added in that special deadpan delivery that was already becoming one of her trademarks. But, the outrage had already been perpetrated—and, besides, after some of the hints she had dropped to them about the Continental, Johnny's viewers were ready for almost anything.

Actually Bette stayed at the Hotel Maryland during that first Chicago engagement, just up Rush Street from Kelly's. She was more nervous about the Kelly's gig than she let "The Tonight Show" viewers know. It was, in a very real sense, her big-time nightclub debut. She had played a place called Paul's Mall in Boston, but Kelly's

was a club of major singnificance, and everyone
knew it. Located in the heart of Chicago's Near
North Side, it was near both the swinging singles
bars and Wells Street, then in the last throes of
folk-rock and hippiedom. But the Kelly's crowd
was seldom either the stewardesses and their one-
night stands or the folkniks from Old Town.
Kelly's was still (and remains so, even today)
hard-core conventioneer and suburbanite. The
closest the crowd got to being young swingers was
when the high school prom crowds hit each
spring, and there were no proms in October.

So Bette was up against a major challenge. Obviously, the gay repartee from the Baths wasn't
going to suffice completely, but she didn't want to
abandon it entirely either. It had become an
identity with her. She felt safe with it.

So the Chicago act was toned down a bit. Not
much: "She still came out singing 'Sh-Boom,' and
jiggling her jugs," as Bruce Vilanch, who had just
moved to Chicago recalls. "She had on this purple
dress and no bra, which was outrageous at the
time, four years ago. People just weren't wearing
no bras onstage then. And she created quite a
sensation with Jackie Vernon's audience, most of
whom had passed away many years ago, of
course." Even Friedman admits that she stole the
show from Vernon. Having conquered Middle
America (not completely, perhaps, but significantly enough that Kelly's brought her back four
times, including twice as headliner), Bette was
more clearly than ever on the road to the stardom
that Friedman and others envisaged for her.

Bette at the Gay Liberation Day Parade, June, 1973. (Photo by Robert Deutsch)

Montage: Bette at the Continental Baths, February 4, 1973. (Photo by Peter Dallas)

Al Fullerton and I flew to Chicago for the Kelly's opening, and, as Al recalls (he had seen her more recently than I had, and at the Baths; at that time I'd only seen her two or three times at the Improv), "she didn't do the Carmen Miranda or the Mae West numbers, just the '50s kind of stuff and some slow things. But it was nothing like the outrageous costuming and the outrageous gestures that she did at the Baths." The first night we were there, she got into a heavy stream-of-consciousness rap about Frederick's of Hollywood. Al remembers the audience loving it: "I guess everybody can identify with that. People in Chicago probably get those catalogs, too, from this guy out in Hollywood pushing his line of padded asses and padded bras. The catalogs don't have photos; they're all drawings, which look like drag queens with about eight wigs on, and falls down to their asses. One of the products was a blow-up bra. You have tubes coming out of each cup and you blow it up to the size you want. Girdles, garters, kicky little high heels. It was very '50s and Bette went on about it forever that night."

After her second show, Bette came to a party at the apartment where Al and I were staying with some Chicago friends, Peter Born and Jon Philips. She was dressed quite simply, in an old black dress ('30s, I think) and what she called her Sonja Henie monkey boa. She was tired after her two shows, and very quiet—though quite concerned about what we thought of the show, how it had compared to the times we had seen her in New

York, etc. After a while we all went back to the all-night restaurant at the Hotel Maryland for breakfast.

After Al and I returned to New York, Peter and Jon met Bette one day the next week for breakfast, a movie (*Five Easy Pieces*), and a trip to a junk clothes shop. "We were wandering around this crowded room full of things," says Jon. "Old furs, laces, beads, bangles, hats. She was trying on things desperately." Really in her element, until, stopping dead in her tracks, she realized she no longer had her Sonja Henie monkey boa.

Eventually it was located in a corner, under some clothes she'd been trying on, but there were some tense moments during the search. "Being a typical New Yorker," Peter adds, "naturally her first thought was that someone had stolen it."

Bette headed back to New York, monkey boa intact, for another eight weeks at the Baths. Then came a second trip to Kelly's, opening for Mort Sahl in May of 1971, during which she managed to shock one of the city's leading stuffed shirts —and to meet the man who was to live with her and to play bass in her band for almost two years.

First, the stuffed shirt incident. As Bruce Vilanch tells it, Irv Kupcinet, Chicago gossip columnist and television talk-show host, has this boat ride each year, called the Purple Heart Cruise, for all the vets from hospitals throughout the Midwest. "They bring them down, and they charter a battleship" (I trust Bruce is not making this up) "and they go out and they sail around all day in the lake. And they feed them and give them door prizes and gifts and there's a big show that goes on all day long."

Talent for the show, of course, is "volunteer." Whoever happens to be playing in town at the time. And you just don't hardly say no to Irv Kupcinet. So Bette agreed.

The problem was the band. "They had no idea what she was doing," Bruce explains. "The band was composed of a lot of guys who were out of work that day. From the musicians union. They didn't care. She got to rehearse with them for about ten minutes. She gave them her charts, and they played everything wrong in rehearsal. So she corrected them and said, 'No, try this, try that.' And they did it. But when she got on, they did it all wrong again. So she turned around and said, 'No, this is the one that goes—' and *sang* it for them. She turned back around to the audience with a smile, and the band did it completely wrong again.

"So finally at the end of the show, she said to the vets, 'I want to thank you all for being such a patient audience. I thought you were wonderful. I'm glad you're having such a wonderful time.' Then she turned around, 'And to this band, I'd only like to say one thing. Fuck you.' And she walked off. They were really stunned, Kup was absolutely startled. So word got around that Bette was a four-letter girl."

Another Chicago television talk-show host figured in Bette's first meeting with Michael Federal, who became her lover and bass player.

"I had just finished doing *Hair* about six months before," Michael says, "and while Bette was working at Mister Kelly's with Mort Sahl, the Kelly's press agent, Bill Wilson, brought her up to the 'Sig Sakowitz Show' for an interview. I happened to be at the station visiting Jim McCloud, who had done Hud in *Hair* and was working there then, and she walked in the door. I knew Bill, because he had done press for *Hair*, too, so I said hello to them both and asked her out."

Bette insisted that Michael come to the show first. He said, "I went and was knocked out. She was very, very good."

Bette and Michael went to the beach together the next day and got along well. Michael had been more or less at loose ends since the closing of *Hair*. ("I don't know whether you know too much about recuperating from doing *Hair*, but there were an awful lot of people who got really turned around by that. I was one of them. Because they took people off the street. They didn't tell you how to act, they just said go ahead and do your thing. So then you got onstage, and I was doing Claude, and I was taking a bad trip and dying eight times a week. And my method of acting was that if I believe it, they'll believe it. After a while I couldn't disconnect. When I walked off the stage, I'd take it home with me. That's not too cool, as I found out.")

Bette lived with Michael for a few weeks in Chicago, then asked him to come back to New York with her. She was forming her first real band at this time, and asked Michael to play bass.

("I was always a singer. I played guitar to accompany myself, or worked as a front man for bands down South. But when I met Bette, what she needed was a bass player. So I said, 'That's all right. I like bass very much.' So I went out and bought a bass and started working on it.")

The new set-up also included Barry Manilow on piano and Kevin Ellman on drums. After a short rehearsal period, Bette and the band were ready for her New York nightclub debut, at the Downstairs at the Upstairs, a small, plush ("intimate" is the polite term) nightclub in mid-Manhattan which usually booked relatively quiet, older stylists like Mabel Mercer or Felicia Saunders.

Bette asked Peter Dallas, who had been touring with Laura Nyro as lighting man and who had become friendly with Bette during the engagement at the Baths, to light her show at the Downstairs. "I said I'd love to," says Dallas. "So I ran over. Naturally it was the eleventh hour. I went down there and she rehearsed for me, and I sort of blocked out the lighting, and made a go of it. And that was the engagement that did it. Because she went in there very insecure, very afraid, and at first she was not very successful. Those first four or five nights were disastrous. And you could count the people, on one hand, who were there." (Lou Miele of *After Dark* likewise recalls the opening nights as almost empty—"a couple of visiting businessmen and their call girls, and she was very hostile to them.")

"So Bette took her own money and put an ad in *Screw* magazine," Dallas continues, referring to New York's leading pornoliberationist tabloid. "It said something about Bette Midler, from the Tubs, being back at the Downstairs. She had to get some of *her* people coming. It was very depressing for all concerned.

"Suddenly on the sixth night—this whole episode is almost like a Hollywood musical—on the sixth night, the place is packed. Standing ovations. People are screaming. People are dying. She's brilliant. The seventh night. They're sitting on the rafters and the wall. It was like, the *crème* is arriving. The John Schlesingers. The Truman Capotes. The Johnny Carsons. The Karen Blacks. The Tom O'Horgans. There they all are."

Through Laura Nyro, Dallas had connections at Columbia Records and got a friend who worked for the label to come down and hear Bette. The friend likewise flipped and, at Dallas's urging, managed to get Clive Davis, then president of Columbia Records, to come down, too.

Davis was, for some reason, "completely unimpressed," Dallas says. "He walked out without even coming backstage. I felt terrible, and of course Bette was wrecked." However, by some weird quirk of fate, the very next night the audience included a stranger in a tuxedo who arrived late and stood at the back of the room. No one in Bette's organization had invited him or knew why he was there, but Ahmet Ertegun, president of Atlantic Records, *did* come backstage after the show—and later offered Bette a very big, very important record contract.

The show Ertegun saw was rather spectacular. It seems (or so Dallas recalls) that a group of hairdressers from Brooklyn—old fans of Bette from the Tubs—had rented out the whole club that night for a private party. "The place was packed. So packed that they literally had to carry her offstage. The audience. And they threw confetti on her. They were standing on the tables. They were screaming. They picked her up like a football star and carried her out of the room.

"Ertegun was floored," Dallas continues. "He was very turned on by the fact that Bette had such a stage presence, and that not only was she a songstress, but she was a personality as well."

Bill Duff-Griffin and Tom Eyen went one night to see Bette at the Downstairs, and she recognized them in the audience and dished them good-naturedly from the stage (they, of course, dished back). After the show, Bill overheard a middle-aged businessman at the next table ask a young Midler fan, "Do you know where she's going after this?"

The young man looked back coolly and replied: "Up. Just *up*."

"Up" included some interesting side trips, as Michael recalls, including a gig in Bermuda. "It rained twelve days out of fourteen. We were working at the Princess Hotel. A convention of pipefitters or something. It was very strange. When we got there, everything was real green, you know, flowers everywhere. Little tiny roads, and small cars. Incredible scenery. Then we found out why it was so green. Because it rains. *All* the time."

Michael talked Bette into her first motorbike ride in Bermuda, however. "She was raised to believe that things could hurt her, you know. Don't try anything because you might get hurt. So she was really scared at first, but once she got on it and started moving around, figured out how it worked, she really had a good time. We had to talk her into it, but she did it."

Once, in New Orleans, Michael recalls, Kevin (the drummer) was reading *The Exorcist*. "He got very freaked out by it and didn't want to stay in his room by himself, so we told him, sure, come on up to our room. So Bette ran and hid behind the curtains, threw a big sheet over her head, and jumped out at him when he walked into the room."

New Orleans was a strange gig. The Blue Room at the Hotel Roosevelt, which made Kelly's look wild and freaky by comparison. "The first night there were like thirteen people there, and it's a big, big room. But it built, it really built for her, chiefly from word of mouth. And at the end of the gig, there were quite a few people there, but it was a hard, hard gig."

That last night the band had gone out and bought masks—"Weird, weird masks. A green mask with strange things hanging out. A devil mask for Barry. And we kept them out of sight, I think, until she started to introduce us at the end of the act. And as she was saying, 'And now ladies and gentlemen, on this end—' she turned around and looked and freaked out. Fell right on the floor. And just as she recovered from it, Bill came waltzing out from the wings in this gorilla mask. She fell on the floor again. Fell right out."

Miss M/Bette continues to emerge as a very lively—and unpredictable—lady, onstage and off.

Then came Vegas. The Congo Room at the Sahara. Opening for Johnny Carson. "The highlight of my stay was the Flamingo sign," Bette was quoted by *Playboy*. "It looked like a big pink orgasm."

"I liked working for him," she said of Carson in *Interview*, "he's very professional." But Las Vegas itself? "Everyone wears wigs. It's a heavy wig town. I got real good reviews, but I had lots of trouble dealing with the audience. I have to have love from an audience. When I feel warmth, then I'm warm."

As Craig Karpel wrote in *Oui*, "Vegas audiences like their *entendres* double. Single *entendres* they consider crude. Single *entendres* delivered by femme songstresses they do not consider. Is it worth $100,000 a week to Bette to stop saying 'tits'?" (It wasn't, thank God.)

At about four o'clock in the morning after opening night in Vegas, Michael and Bette were up in their room, already in bed, when the telephone rang. It was Fayette Hauser, one of San Francisco's famous Cockettes, whom Bette had hired to be her dresser during the Vegas run. She was, first of all, a day late. Besides that, she was in jail, having gotten busted by the police as soon as she stepped off the plane.

Why? As Michael puts it, "I guess it was mostly because of the way she was dressed. She had like three dresses on. They like to put on layers of clothing. And a weird hat with all kinds of birds in it. Bracelets up to her armpits. And in her hair, she also had tied two baby shoes. Anyway, she was in jail. What was her line? Great line. 'Hit in the face with the pie of reality.' "

Michael and Bette told Faye to get some sleep, that they would get her out in the morning. Free again, she arrived at their room with two enormous trunks: "As soon as she got into the room, she opened up the trunks and the trunks proceeded to explode all over the room. She had one trunk full of nothing but hats and shoes. The other trunk was full of dresses and stuff." All things for Bette to wear onstage. In Las Vegas, that heavy wig town (Bette freaked people out by just walking through the casinos with curlers in her hair). Bette ended up wearing "maybe a string of beads and a belt with rhinestone pins on it. That was all, out of those two trunks."

One afternoon, Michael and Bette went horseback riding and Faye came along. "And she was a mess, a complete mess. Big silver go-go boots. Some black outfit. All this on horseback. It was an incredible sight."

Bette returned to New York to play The Bitter End immediately after Vegas. A leading folk showcase in the late '50s and early '60s, the club made a rather uncomfortable (but financially successful) switch to hard rock in the late '60s—and was thus another steppingstone for Bette in determining just how broad her appeal was going to be.

She came out in gold-lamé pedal-pushers and a black corset, "The cups are B and I'm D," she announced, and then insisted that she'd ripped the outfit off the back of Ann-Margret out in Vegas.

Bette had the patter in perfect control by this time. "Just the outfit was worth waiting in the rain for, wasn't it? I wasn't going to wear my gold lamé, I was just going to wear my red pants . . . It's hard to find spike heels as tacky as the ones I have on . . . My booking agents simply do *not* know where to send me. Would you believe Las Vegas? Lost Wages, I called it. Everyone, absolutely everyone there is fat . . . This song is not old, but it sounds like it is . . . Here's another blasto from the pasto, something to make you mash-potato once again . . . Don't worry, I shake my tits a lot. If you don't want to listen you can just watch . . . Have you seen the subways lately? The graffiti? That Taki 183, you know, that child is a genius. Can you imagine some little girl down there with her magic marker writing Kotex 142? I'd just freak. It used to be you'd ask kids what their name was, now it's what's your number . . . In this next number, I'm going to use my tough *shiksa* voice . . . This group is so handsome. I wish you could see it from where I am, it's just cruise, cruise, cruise."

Miss M was together. Outrageous. Wonderful. These were heavy rock hipsters at The Bitter End, but she could just as well have been back at the Baths with that last remark. The image was set, and there was no changing it, no compromising it —for the straights or the swingers.

4. enter aaron the baron

from carnegie to philharmonic halls

The night I saw Bette at The Bitter End, I was surprised to see two old acquaintances in the first row, right in front of the stage: Aaron Russo and his wife Andrea.

Russo had been owner/operator of the Kinetic Playground, a large rock palace in Chicago. He was a wheeler-dealer from the word go, but he ran a good club, and I believe he ran it fairly and honestly, despite some grumblings to the contrary from some of the artists who performed there (and to be frank, those were the days when you had to take the constant money grumblings of *nouveau riche* performers with a grain of salt). I know he did more for bringing important rock music to Chicago than any other person. He was, furthermore, quite knowledgeable about the artistic side of the industry, as well as the business aspects of rock. He knew who to book, and he got them.

Russo was not, however, the kind of person you'd ask over for dinner on a Tuesday night. Or go out with for a drink after the show. Or run to introduce your dates to. He was always friendly to me, and we got along relatively well. But there was always the hint of caution in the air: He was being pleasant to me because it was politic to be pleasant to the only regular rock writer (at that time) on one of the city's dailies. I knew why he was being pleasant, and he knew I knew.

I neither liked him nor disliked him. (I did rather like Andrea, whom I always found very warm and congenial and nicely unaffected by the rockstar rat race and personality squabbles that were always going on backstage.) But, I did respect Aaron. He did what he did efficiently and well. As wheeler-dealers go, he's certainly the best choice of many that I can think of. Her chart says that Bette needed a wheeler-dealer, a strong, almost dictatorial business manager to anchor her through the storms. Absolutely. So I guess it was in the stars.

Russo, who was at that time dividing his time between New York and Chicago, first started expressing a serious interest in Bette's career about the time of The Bitter End. Bette then played Mister Kelly's in Chicago again in May 1972, just prior to her big date at Carnegie Hall. But, it wasn't until she returned to Kelly's that September that Aaron really made his move.

At that time, Bette was being managed by Artists Entertainment Complex, Inc., working primarily with Norman Weiss and Michael Liebert. According to Bill Hennessy, she was not exactly crazy with the way they had been handling her career (they came into the picture about the time of the Downstairs at the Upstairs engagement and had advised Bette to pursue the lucrative Las Vegasy hotel-room circuit, a course which she wisely objected to). But Bette's career began to take off quickly in the summer of '72, and by the time Aaron was officially installed as her personal manager that September (curiously enough, with AEC's blessings, as things worked out), he had a piece of very hot property indeed.

Bette Midler was not the first outrage to hit New York's hallowed hall of Carnegie. Best known for its classical music programs, Carnegie had been experimenting with popular entertainment for a few years, first with folk singers and jazz artists, then on to big-business rock. The smell of marijuana had more than once wafted up toward the chandeliers.

Nonetheless, Bette's Carnegie Hall concert was an *event*—very fashionable, very hip, very gay. All the rock cognoscenti of New York were there, dressed to the teeth. The "word" that had started at The Bitter End had now gotten around: Bette Midler was a good place to be for the vanguard-

declarers in those last few days before the annual
Fire Island exodus that summer.

Bette's act had acquired one major change: She
had gotten her first back-up trio, three girls in
long prom gowns, whom she called the Celestial
Choir—M-G-M, an acronym of the three women's
first names, Melissa, Gail, and Merle.

Melissa Manchester stayed with the group
through Philharmonic Hall, on December 31st of
that year, then launched out on her own career as
a performer/songwriter. Gail Kantor and Merle
Miller (the latter name usually drew chuckles
from many of Bette's gay audiences, since it was
the same as that of a writer who had written a
whiny "true confession" revelation of his homosexuality—in *The New York Times Magazine*, yet
—about a year earlier) stayed with the Midler
entourage through the following April (the end of
the first big coast-to-coast tour).

By Philharmonic Hall, the girls had become the
Harlettes and had acquired a considerably different image than that presented in their Carnegie
Hall debut. "We were unprepared at Carnegie
Hall," says Gail, "in terms of character. We
weren't dressed right. We just didn't fit the part,
but it was thrown together so quickly that it was
hard to expect much else. And, I didn't really
understand what she wanted of us up there, as a
part of that show."

Bette had seen Melissa perform at clubs like
Folk City and Larry Bresner's Focus on 74th
Street (Bresner, who later became Melissa's hus-
band and manager, once had turned Bette down

for a singing gig at his club, back in the days
before she played the Continental). Melissa in
turn recommended Gail, whom Bette knew
slightly, because the three of them all studied with
the same voice teacher, David Collier. Merle was
a friend of Barry Manilow.

Melissa is Bronx-born, the daughter of a bas-
soonist with the Metropolitan Opera orchestra.
She graduated from New York's High School of
the Performing Arts and studied songwriting at
New York University with Paul Simon.

Now off on her own career, she is plagued by
comparisons with Bette, a subject that she is reportedly rather supersensitive about. Yet, in performance the similarities *are* striking, both in
terms of body attitudes and vocal style. Both singers move with intense energy, taking fast little
baby steps; both clench their fists, point their index fingers for emphasis, bump and grind a lot,
shake their breasts. They even grimace alike. Vocally, they both sing with a throaty rasp, and play
around with rapid changes in tempo and dynam-
ics. Both speak with a clipped, brisk articulation,
and they have a particular brand of soul that
might be termed Late '60s New York City Jewish.

The point is they *are* singers in a similar tradition—and they are also singers who worked together closely for a six-month period that was
very formative in terms of both their careers. Why
shouldn't there be similarities? (There are also
differences. Melissa's chief talent is as a songwriter, and she's a good one.) And who's to say
that Melissa copied Bette? It could have just as

easily been the other way around, especially in light of the fact that Bette's own act onstage has grown consistently fuller since the addition of the Harlettes.

Gail says, "Certain people are natural mimics. And I think Bette is one. And I think Melissa is, too. And when you hang around your friends for a long time, you pick up similar mannerisms. And people know you're friends, after a while. You don't even have to tell them that you hang out together. I would say that from spending a lot of time together, all of us, every single one of us that would be in the room, would see things that each individual would do, and some things are very contagious."

Gail likewise is New York born (Brooklyn) and Jewish. Having seen Bette perform only on the Carson show (she was not particularly impressed—"It was a method of communicating that I hadn't seen. Her schtick put me off"), she went to see her in person (with Melissa and Larry) at the Downstairs. They went upstairs during the break between shows, and the three girls jammed ("I got to know her a little bit, but it's hard to get to know Bette").

Prior to Carnegie, Bette asked Melissa and Gail to lunch one day ("At Wolfe's Delicatessen, Sixth Avenue and 57th Street. We had soup"). She said that the Carnegie date had been set and asked them if they would consider doing back-up for her. Gail recalls Bette being surprised when they agreed. " 'You mean you would do that?' she said.

'You would sing background for me? But you're both solo performers.' "

At any rate, the arrangements were made. Merle also was asked, and the three began work with Bette and Barry immediately. Miss M now had some lady friends with her up onstage, to counterpoint her in camp and to help her dish out the dirt.

Carnegie Hall was a decided success for Bette (with almost everyone in the sold-out house, that is: Lou Miele of *After Dark* recalls how he had to hush a group of noisy older people in the same box where he was sitting, only to find out that one of them was Bette's aunt from New Jersey). The next New York appearance was probably the biggest triumph to date—singing under the stars in the middle of Central Park, at the Schaefer Festival in the Wollman Rink Theater there.

"When I heard the roar I thought I was in *Korea*!" Bette told Lisa Robinson for her *Interview* interview. "Entertaining the troops . . . I really did. I walked out and I said, *this is Korea*! That concert was the happiest night of my life. I could feel it inside, I could feel the joy . . . really physically; it was like a big *lump* in my *chest* and it was coming OUT in huge WAVES."

She told *Cash Box:* "I had my girls there, and my girls were dressed up for the first time. They're such great trash, the harlots. They're pretty funky girls and they like to shake their tail feathers a little. So we got them in spiked heels and tight dresses and had a great time."

Tony Finstrom recalls a trek late that same summer to Paramus, New Jersey, where Bette was playing the Bergen Mall: "Seriously. There was this theater in the shopping center. She was there from Tuesday night to Sunday, or something. I had two people visiting me, two girls from Michigan who had never seen her before. They had a car, so I suggested that we drive out to see her.

"It was a small crowd, so she was very casual. She came out in this midnight blue velvet evening gown, very simple, very chic-looking, stunning, like I've never seen her before. Or since. Very simple and striking. And she just let loose.

"When we left, the two girls were trembling. They stayed a couple of weeks in New York and saw a lot of shows, but Bette was like scarred in their minds. They couldn't believe her. They'll never forget her. They'd never seen anything like it before. Coming from Michigan, they didn't know what camp was. They were into a kind of Big Brother and the Holding Company kind of rock scene. Big rock groups.

"But they'd never seen anything like her. They were trembling. They were speechless. If I'd seen her for the first time that night, I would have been speechless, too. She was just unbelievable. Just a three-man back-up group, drums, piano, and bass. But she was incredible."

"Aaron (Baron Bruiso) Russo is the most voluptuous manager to be found today and is the very proud possessor of the most unsavory reputation in show biz," wrote Bette in the Palace program notes, concluding with "Mr. Russo and The Divine have been together since September 1972, and are completely exhausted by the intensity of their relationship but completely fulfilled as well." The reference is perhaps to their widely touted affair-beyond-business-affairs, which was often stormy and which had by that time pretty much run its course.

Gail Kantor recalls first meeting Aaron when Bette and the girls were rehearsing for Mister Kelly's in late summer of 1972: "We had rented a studio downtown, called Baggies. Aaron's the kind of person who has a very strong image of himself—a very strong, macho image—and he really was seeking to ingratiate himself to the band and the girls. He really wanted Bette as a client. He was almost too friendly. But she *really* trusted him. She trusted him probably more so because he cared for her so deeply."

By the time the girls got to Chicago (Bette did one week at Kelly's alone that September, then brought the Harlettes in for the second week), negotiations were hot and heavy with Russo. "Aaron was about," as Bruce Vilanch puts it. "Aaron was conspicuous by his presence . . ."

Russo, who's Jewish and from New York, had started his career in the ladies' underwear business. He was associated with New York's Electric Circus for a while before moving to Chicago and opening his own expensive multi-media palace, which he renamed the Kinetic Playground after the New York owners of the Electric Circus threatened suit over the name he originally

picked, the Electric Theatre. Press at the time of
the Playground's opening promised a full dose of
the hip mystique—gurus, astrologers, Indian
dance, etc. Most of that never panned out, but the
hall became known for its live rock, its whirla-
round stereo system, and its psychedelic slide-film-
lighting effects.

Russo kept the Playground open through most
of 1968 and 1969, and the facilities had begun to
fray a bit around the edges by the end (one person from Chicago that I interviewed recalls it as
"that slinky, sleazy Kinetic Playground," and I
remember things having gotten into a rather ad-
vanced state of disrepair by the time I moved to
New York in May 1969). After that, Russo had
gone into management (including a Chicago rock
group called the Flock) without much success.

So he was ready to make his move to manage
Bette (Bill Hennessy calls it "the grand play").
The problem, of course, was that Bette already
had a management agency, Artists Entertainment
Complex.

So, according to Hennessy, Aaron convinced
Bette to write a letter to AEC, asking a release.
She did, and AEC replied with a court summons,
which was delivered to Miss M onstage at Kelly's
(she thought it was a letter from a fan and accepted it with a joke).

"The next five days were the most painful in
her life," Bill recalls. "All these people, David
Geffen, Ahmet Ertegun, all the people were calling, telling her, Bette, absolutely under no cir-

cumstances should you go and get involved with Aaron Russo."

Gail says: "I realize now the pressure she was undergoing. Because here they had completed, had pretty much completed the album. It was in the remixing stages. And Ahmet didn't want Aaron to manage Bette. He just didn't like Aaron. And so he tried to influence her. And here she was being spoken to by a very heavy man in the record industry, long distance, telling her not to do something that she wanted to do very badly. And the record isn't out yet. And she still did what she wanted to do. She was on the verge of exploding career-wise, whether she knew it or not. She could have destroyed herself."

Then came the surprise (which is maybe not such a surprise knowing Russo): Aaron works out a deal with AEC so that he not only gets to manage Bette, but, as Hennessy puts it: "He even gets his office there and comes out with a nice percentage. An office, a phone. He did *remarkably*. He *came in*. The album had already been finished. I mean it was amazing. You've got to give it to him. That's being a shrewd business-man."

Reactions to Aaron's new influence were varied. There was immediate tension with Hennessy, who in the absence of any strong management in Bette's career prior to Aaron, had exhibited considerable influence on Bette both personally and professionally. "Aaron came into the picture," Bill says, "and became, to be kind, overbearing. In terms of being the kind of manager who closes the door and locks Barry and I out so we couldn't even get in half the time to discuss what was going to go on before the show."

"Anyway, I left," Hennessy continues. "It was very painful for both Bette and me because we had been together for such a long time. It was emotional, but I had to go. Aaron did very well by making me leave, in a way, because he made me go on my own, made me decide to work with other people, but it was very emotional.

"Aaron wanted Bette for himself. He had to operate on that level. Some managers have to. I don't operate on that level, but I can see his point.

"I think he's done well, for what needs she had. I think it will be interesting to see what he does now. Because let's say, that on an average scale of one to a hundred, Aaron came in at eighty-five. The album was already done, the following had been built, she had been pushed mainly by herself. Her managerial agency didn't do beans except, you know, put up the money. But *now*, this is where Aaron has to come in and really prove himself. And the next step has to be something really good. They can't find the script, the director, the movie they want to choose because they're so afraid, and Aaron doesn't really know, does he? Because if he did know, he'd have it right at his fingertips. Now he's earning his money, he's *really* earning his bread, if he knows who to pick and how to be a good producer.

"I think the thing that upsets me about Aaron is his ego, which is enormous. The need to have his name *above*. You know, so many things like that.

But that's the name of the game, so on the other hand, I can't put him down for it. Some people need that.

"I personally take Aaron for what he is. There were points when I didn't get along with him, there were points when I did get along with him. But, you have to learn to accept people. Some people say he's a killer. He discounts human beings so much, on one level; and on another, I think he gets guilt feelings about it. The man is very complex. His strategy forces are enormous.

"I'm not a fan of his, by any stretch of the imagination, but I accept him for what he is. He has undermined, he has done things to all of us, that, you know, I wouldn't say are either nice or bad. It's just business practices that I wouldn't operate on."

Michael Federal, whose personal relationship with Bette was also complicated by Russo's appearance on the scene, praises Aaron for his "stick-to-it-ivity" in looking out for Bette's interests. "He's a strange man. At the time, I said, 'Yeah, I think it would be a great idea for you to go with him as a manager.' And I think he has been incredible for her. He's got her a lot of work. As a businessman, he's a tiger, a fucking tiger. I think he is a good businessman. But there's more to business than business. I'm not a good businessman. I can't comment on that. I think he's a good man, that he's got it in him to be a good man. And he loved her, that's for sure."

Gail says, "Bette really trusted Aaron, and I

think her decision was correct. He's been a hell of a manager, very good for her career."

Of the people around Bette that I spoke to, Gail was almost alone in saying she liked Russo personally. "I do like him, and I think that he likes me. He knows that I know where he's coming from. He knows that I know when he's full of shit. When you're a businessman you have to deal with all these people, and you have to have the upper hand, for some reason or the other.

"When I got back from a trip to California and wanted to see Bette at the Palace in December, I called up his office. His secretary said there were absolutely zilch tickets. None at all. She said if they had one, I would have it. And I said fine, and forgot about it.

"And a half hour later, Aaron himself calls me. Takes a few minutes out to call me. A ticket was just freed, he said. Somebody wasn't able to go that night. That was a really nice gesture from him. He could've called a lot of people. But he called me."

Former rock publicist Michael Goldstein, the founder of the *Soho Weekly News* in New York, knew Russo when he was booking some of Goldstein's clients (Jimi Hendrix, Led Zeppelin) into Chicago: "I've always had a high respect for Aaron. He was one of the few managers who would call me up and say, I need publicity because one of your people is coming through town. What do you want me to do, etc. He was always a very open man to getting the job done. A real good business guy. And I always liked him as a person. He was always very straight on the phone, very straight when I met him. He knew what the bullshit was, and what was the truth."

Aaron quickly started to work on Bette's image —to get her more dates like The Bitter End, on the hip-rock circuit that he knew best. "Aaron tried to bring Bette's image to another place in terms of straight people," Hennessy recalls, "but the ironic part about it was that straight people were ready for that gay thing now. That's why Aaron didn't change the material, why the same act was brought to the Palace. Aaron realized by then that there was a whole middle class of people from the Bronx and Forest Hills who were ready to enjoy her." As Craig Karpel observed in a rather good article on Bette in *Oui Magazine*, Bette was, "the first performer in history to tour the provinces with the open expectation that the Gay gate would crack the nut and leave the straights for gravy, would tear the open door of The Closet off its hinges and dance on it."

So Aaron booked Bette into the Troubador in Los Angeles (with songwriter Peter Allen), the Boarding House in San Francisco (where she broke house records and shared the bill with Alex Harvey, the composer of one of her best pieces of material, "Delta Dawn"), and the Club Bijou in Philadelphia.

Then back to New York for another biggie: New Year's Eve at Philharmonic Hall. Bette had made it all the way from singing for free at the Improv to selling out two full houses in one of the large prestigious halls in New York's culture complex, Lincoln Center for the Performing Arts.

"I hope you stay with me," Bette told the cheering crowd at Philharmonic Hall, "even when I don't always do what you want me to. Next year you won't even recognize me." The crowd was a bit puzzled by Bette's announcement of a planned image change, her first public statement of a growing dissatisfaction with the camp image of the Divine Miss M—an image that she had created, that was certainly initially a part of her own personality, but which now even she had begun to feel had gotten out of hand. There were immediate cries that this meant Bette was going to abandon her gay following, like Barbra Streisand and Roberta Flack before her, but the reference seems to have been more in terms of wanting to broaden her range of material, not limit her audience in any way. And here again, Russo was possibly a prime influence, though whether there was a real agreement between Bette and Aaron as to which direction her "broadening" should take is probably debatable.

Meanwhile, the Philharmonic concert itself was the ultimate madcap romp. Bette's first entrance was in a sedan chair, carried onstage by six men in khaki. After the intermission, Bette arose from the orchestra pit, wearing only a New Year's baby diaper and singing "Auld Lang Syne." The Harlettes were quite together by this time, and the audience simply went wild.

"The girls were really incorporated into the act by then," Al Fullerton recalls. "During 'Higher

Liza Minnelli and Bette tête-à-tête at the 1974 Tony Awards.
(Photo by Frank Teti)

Aaron Russo and Bette at the After Dark Ruby Awards in
1973, when Bette was named Entertainer of the Year. (Photo
by Robert Morris)

Johnny Carson and Bette at the 1974 Tony Awards. (Photo by Frank Teti)

and Higher,' they were all over the stage, really enjoying themselves. Bette's voice wasn't at its best that night, but she made it into one of the most fantastic evenings ever. Sparklers in the audience, firecrackers, and all that dope being passed. She seemed as if she considered it her own special little house party. You know, get up and dance, have a ball, it's New Year's Eve.

"And then the baby diaper! What I remember most about that is that while she was still in the orchestra pit before the platform started being raised up to stage level, she started giggling and saying things under her breath. It was almost like *The Exorcist*, this freaky voice she was using. Slight little giggles of anticipation of what was going to happen in the next few seconds. It was really eerie. Fascinating. And then she gave the countdown and came up and sang 'Auld Lang Syne,' in her diaper and banner saying 1973." Which was to be, without question, the year of Bette Midler.

Aaron Russo was omnipresent during that next year of Bette's career, from Philharmonic Hall to the Palace, and his presence was not always appreciated by those around her. Charlotte Crossley, who replaced Melissa as a Harlette just after Philharmonic, recalls: "When he was around, everybody was kind of like uptight, and when he left, everybody was having a good time, really into Bette, into making her feel good and to keeping her in good spirits. Which is not to say that he wasn't into keeping her in good spirits. But there was a great deal of tension, a great deal of anxiety when he was around.

"He was always friendly, but it was really, really hard to get to know him as a person. But I tried. I remember when we were at the Palace, I hurt my leg, pulled the tendon in my right leg, and it was really painful. And he carried me out to the limousine. Himself. He was a really, really sweet person. But, as a business person, well, I would not like to work with him. I would not like someone like him to manage me.

"But for Bette he was good. They've got a real crazy thing going, and it worked for both of them. He's protective of her, I think a little overprotective. It's real hard to say.

"I like Aaron, he's a good businessman, but he's also a very lonely person, too. He's got a very heavy personal life. But he has had his successes. And he was in *love* with Bette. Buying her incredible things. Giving her mink coats and all that. It's just hard to say. It's difficult.

"They fought a great deal. There was a personal relationship, of course, other than just a manager/client thing. Which got in the way. Got in the way of Bette, because if she wanted to go out and be with somebody, it was very difficult because when Aaron was around, she was with him. He was still married, still is, to the blonde.

"It was very, very difficult because they would fight. It made Bette very unhappy when they fought, which was usually away from the theater, away from working. He was very very jealous, and very very possessive.

"He could not control the Divine Miss M. Or Bette Midler. The two personalities in the one person. Because when Bette went onstage, that magic just was there, that magic that people are talking about is no longer in theater. Some people just have that magic inside of them and can make it happen. She's one of the few people I've seen that can always make it happen. It never failed.

"He could not control that. He had no control over that part of her. He handled all the business, the box office, and made sure she got places on time. But he couldn't control that. And that's why he fell in love with her."

But perhaps Bette herself should have the final word. She told Warren Hoge of *The New York Times* in 1978: "Many people think our relationship is unhealthy. As a matter of fact, most of them do. But Aaron thinks I'm the greatest thing that ever walked, and he did when nobody else did. He's not personally graceful, but he does what he thinks is best for me. Sometimes he's wrong, but most of the time he's right. I'm the only person he has. Who else is there on the market who has that? I consider myself very lucky to have someone who devotes all of his energies and time to my career. Why would I dump that? Who am I going to get? Some nice New York lawyer with 150 clients? I can quarrel with Aaron's methods. I fight with him all the time. But some of our work has been very good work. Some of it has been work that no other two people could do together. He knows how to present me, and he knows the timing and the ticket prices and who's going to come and what it's going to mean for me and when to push me this way and when to push me that way, all of which I know nothing about. We play pretty terrible games with each other, but in its way it's a good relationship."

Nonetheless, in the spring of 1979, the ax fell: Bette fired Aaron Russo, after six-and-a-half stormy years. The woman who had made herself a star (albeit with a little help from her friends) had decided to guide her course alone into the next phase of her career. Whatever happened with *The Rose* and Bette Midler, moviestar, Aaron the Baron wouldn't be around to blame.

5. band on the run

bette and the harlettes hit their stride

Charlotte Crossley (her friends pronounce the first
name as in "Char*low*, lowest of the low") is a tall,
dark and handsome soul sister from the south side
of Chicago. Her credits include being voted the
most talkative in high school; singing in church
("It was a very bourgeois, ste-*rile* church,
though") and getting into some real gospel-shout-
ing later ("I kept listening to all those choirs of
twelve thousand dark divas, thumpin' and
jumpin' and, you know, givin' you lots of wigs
and breasts and robes"); growing up on Brecht
and Weill, Motown and Gogi Grant; seeing lots
of entertainment ("When I was growing up, my
grandmother was into taking us to little culture
things a lot, plays and all, so I really got into
being fascinated with all that, seeing how things

worked"); and acting, first in the Jewish Council Youth Center Drama Group in her Hyde Park (University of Chicago) neighborhood, then in *Hair* (in Chicago and on the road) before going on to New York and the Great White Way, in *Jesus Christ Superstar* ("I was a soul girl, a leper, and I came out of the sky on a butterfly") and a short-lived *commedia dell' arte* musical called *Tricks*. Then surrogate superstardom as the lowest of the low, the sleaziest of the sleazy, the Harlette to end all Harlettes, establishing a reputation that is not likely to be soon forgotten.

Charlotte hit New York in August 1971. Her first exposure to Bette came on television, at about that time. "I'd been in the city about two or three weeks," she recalls. "A lot of my gay friends were telling me about her, how fabulous she was, and this and that. And before all this, they were telling me how much like her I was, and I had no idea who this woman *was*, or anything. They said, you talk like her, you're outrageous. And this was just when I was getting into the whole antique-clothes experience, so I was copping an attitude with that, but I didn't know anything about her. Then I saw her on TV, and I was kind of moved. It was on 'The Johnny Carson Show,' where she did this whole thing with the soda fountain, with her in a black leather jacket and spiked heels. 'Leader of the Pack.' She was pretty far out. But then, I sort of passed it off. I said, yeah, yeah, yeah. But everybody in New York was screaming over her."

A short time later, Charlotte met Bette at a

party thrown by the company manager of *Hair*. Bette arrived with Michael Federal, whom Charlotte hadn't seen since they were in *Hair* together in Chicago: "I flipped out. There he was, and there was this girl with him, who was like very quiet, if you can believe that, a real quiet girl. And I looked at her and he said, 'This is Bette,' and I said, 'Did I just see you on TV!' And she said, 'Yeah, yeah.'

"We became fast friends. We were talking just as fast as we could, and she said, 'You're just like me,' and I went, 'People are telling me I'm just like *you*.' And she said, 'There are a lot of things similar about us.' And we started talkin' and talkin'."

This first meeting was during the heyday of the Baths. Charlotte started going every Saturday night to see Bette there (getting in on Bette's guest list in the days before women were regularly admitted for the shows). "I got to know this whole group of people. Bill Hennessy, Larry Paulette and all. Just this whole *group*. And then the bigger and bigger she got, I just kept goin'. I almost never missed a weekend."

Their offstage friendship continued as well: "The thing that I was so moved about when I first met her was that she was a person, and the more I got to know her, the closer we became as friends. I really knew, I really understood that what she was doing was one of the hardest things anybody can do in the business."

When Charlotte got in *Superstar*, Bette and Michael came to see her one night and came backstage after the show. "I remember Liza Minnelli was backstage the same night, and Ben Vereen. She and Bette knew each other. It was like diva to diva."

Charlotte had left *Superstar* for *Tricks*. When Bette approached her about replacing Melissa as a Harlette: "This was two days before *Tricks* was supposed to open, which was a week before it closed. Anyway, Bette came to see me. And asked me would I be a Harlette. I said, sure, not knowing the show was going to close. So the show opens, and I called up the next day and there was a notice on the board about the closing, and I go, 'Wow, this is really, the thing I call'—I'm a Buddhist you know—'and this is like the thing we call *myoho*, a kind of balancing effect.' The show was closing—and I had a job."

Charlotte had seen the Harlettes the previous September, at Mister Kelly's in Chicago, while home on a visit. "I checked them out, you know, and they were real cool. They were like very bland white girls, in a way, but kind of great. Bette kept screamin' at them, telling them to get an attitude. I thought they were really slick, but bland, I mean, like blander than the Ronettes. It was nice, because they all had dark hair, and they all looked alike, and they were real cute, but they were real quiet. They *sounded* great, of course. They had all been studio singers, and they sounded great."

Melissa worked closely with Charlotte, teaching her all the parts. The transition was smooth and amicable. Charlotte firmly contests Ed McCormack's contention in his *Rolling Stone* profile of Bette that there were a lot of hard feelings about Melissa's leaving: "That article was just poisonous, really unfair. I think Melissa made a very graceful exit. Bette really, really loves Melissa. She's very proud of her. The only person who might have been spreading any sort of poisonous conflict was Aaron, because he had a way of doing that."

Melissa had been Charlotte's favorite Harlette ("I noticed her because she had the most personality"), and they worked together easily during the changeover. "We just got right down and started singing the songs together. Melissa left me with great feelings and really taught me a lot about the music. I got to know her pretty well. It's funny, because a lot of people say that she's a lot like Bette. Vocally, they go to the same voice teacher, and they do have little things in their voices that are similar, I think. But they're not at all alike, personality-wise. Melissa is a very cooled-out, calm person."

After learning the parts from Melissa, Charlotte started working with Gail and Merle. "A whole different attitude sort of came over us," Merle says. Gail concurs: "Charlotte really did help my performing. Merle and I both loosened up quite a bit after she came along, and Bette knew this would happen because Charlotte's a *performer*. Charlotte's *out*, you know." Liberation continues to mushroom.

Bette's first "real" tour (she had been "on the road" previously, both with and without her band, but this was the first city-by-city, one-night-stand-then-on-the-next-one trek) started in Rochester, New York, in February 1973. It took Bette, the band (Dicky Frank on guitar, Luther Rix on drums, and Michael Federal on bass, plus Manilow on piano), and the Harlettes around the country for about two months, hitting some thirty different cities.

"We were a very family-oriented group," says Gail. "Maybe it should have been a little more professional, but I'll always remember that tour." (Gail also has very fond memories of the date at Mr. Kelly's that she and Merle and Melissa did with Bette the previous September: "I think that's really my fondest memory. We shared a suite with Bette, and we'd all get stoned and very giddy after the show. Bette never really partook, though. She remained somewhat apart. She was very serious-minded at the time. I think she's always pretty serious-minded. She doesn't take things lightly.")

The opening date in Rochester went well, though Gail had just gotten out of the hospital the week before and was still feeling pretty miserable. "But it went really well," she recalls. "It was the first sign of what kind of a crowd we would get outside New York City, and it was a very mixed crowd, not heavily gay. Freaks. Middle-class people. Everyone."

Other observers were less prone to discount the gay element in the out-of-town audiences. Craig Karpel described a concert in Buffalo, New York, with: "The gaiety was contagious. I found myself laughing with relief at being privileged to relate to all that male pulchritude, flaunted shamelessly for the first time in a civic-auditorium lobby instead of some dank meatrack. Years, centuries of dissimulation, guilt, and blackmail would come to a symbolic end that night in Buffalo."

Bill Hennessy was still very much a leading member of the entourage at this time, despite growing tensions with Russo. Part of his job was to gear Bette's jokes to each locale of the tour. (The audiences particularly loved it when her insults really got personal in terms of local persons and places. They worked somewhat in the nature of in-jokes shared against the outside world.) Karpel points out that in Buffalo, Bette's patter contained several references, in particular, to the homosexual underground in that city: "When she quipped about the local bartender/matchmaker, one Mother Bruce, she brought the house down around the uncomprehending straight majority, and for the first time in Buffalo the tables were turned, it was the heteros' turn to feign guffaws at a gay gag . . . Bette uses an old vaudeville trick to cater to the gays. She and her comedy writer tailor the act's giggles to incorporate references to the gay scene wherever she works. 'Took a walk down *Chippewa*,' she says slyly in Buffalo. The boys bounce in their seats with delight. Mamma *knows*, fellows."

Putting down other places ("I just played a date in Troy, New York," she told an audience in Passaic, New Jersey. "It was like a big hockey

rink") was also popular, as well as bitchy one-
liners directed at such non-hip public figures as
Tricia Nixon ("I just sent her a man-eating plant
for a wedding present. I thought maybe she might
learn something from it." Dear Tricia has just
married a man named Cox . . .) or performer/
competitors ("I can't believe I'm on the same
stage where Karen Carpenter got her drums
banged," or "Ms. Reddy? She *should* be singing 'I
Am Woman.' Who could tell?").

And the self-put-downs, of course, created a
sense of empathy as well, especially with audiences who, for whatever reason, had thought of
themselves as outcasts: "I'm everything you are
afraid your little girls, and little boys, too, will
grow up to be." Or already have grown up to be.

Still, Gail Kantor is right. It wasn't *just* the
gays, or just the young rebels, or just the freaks
who turned out. Bill Marvel of *The National Observer* began his piece describing Bette's appearance in Milwaukee, Wisconsin, with the following
description: "Somebody's grandmother is standing at the head of the line, chattering across at
least two generation gaps to a girl in scruffy blue
jeans. 'Oh, I've watched her on "The Johnny Carson Show". I didn't even tell my friends who I'm
coming to see.' With derision, '*They've* never
heard of her.' " Exiles on Main Street come in all
shapes, sizes, colors, and ages.

Gail told Bette at the end of the tour (in San
Francisco) that she wanted to leave and pursue
her own songwriting career. She has done so now

since her departure, building up an impressive repertory of her own songs, and is presently uncertain as to whether or not she wants to get back into the performing rat race.

Merle also decided to leave the group following the tour, which meant the end of the original Harlettes. By this time, also, Barry was the only remaining member of Bette's original band. Michael Federal had been replaced by Will Lee on bass. Guitarist Dicky Frank had left and was followed by Frank Vento. Drummer Luther Rix was now senior member of the onstage entourage (except Barry), having been with the band since Kevin Ellman's departure prior to Philharmonic Hall. Don Grolnick has joined the group as organist.

Charlotte was to remain as the mainstay of the new back-up trio which Bette assembled in midsummer to rehearse for the grueling four-month tour that was to lead to the Palace.

In June, though, Charlotte took off for the Spoleto Festival in Italy, to act for Paul Sills's Story Theater in *Metamorphoses*. The trek was with the understanding that she would return anytime Bette called her: "She even loaned me some money to go to Spoleto. And I told her, 'Bette, if you ever need anything, don't hesitate to call. I'll come right back.' So, about three days before I was to leave Spoleto for Rome, I got this telegram, and it says, 'Please call me collect or be back to New York by July twenty-third.' So I call and call and call and can't get her. So, I sent a telegram, that cost me twenty dollars, saying, 'I

love you. I miss you. I'll be back on the twenty-
second and I'll call you. Can't wait to work with
you again.' "

Meanwhile, Bette was auditioning some seventy
singers to find replacements for Gail and Merle.
She and Barry finally picked Robin Grean, a
pixyish white girl who had been in *Superstar* with
Charlotte, and a second black singer, Sharon
Redd. The combination was to create a magic
onstage that almost equaled that of Miss M herself.

Will Lee's Palace program notes on Robin
Grean insist that she likes to milk cows, that her
name is synonymous with "tasteful" (a kindly insult in the Midler world, of course) and that she's
Episcopalian.

Robin had seen Bette backstage at *Superstar* a
couple of times, but, like Charlotte, she first saw
her perform on the Carson show: "I had no idea
who she was. When she walked out, I said, 'Who
is that *ridiculous*-looking woman? I mean, how
dare she walk out and look like that!' I mean, she
was much heavier, much weirder in the beginning. Then she started to sing, and I thought she
was fabulous, I just thought she was *fabulous*.
There was something about her. I didn't think the
audience was relating to her that much, but I
really liked her a lot. She sang Joni Mitchell's
'For Free,' about the clarinet player."

Robin then saw Bette again at David Collier's
studio (where she, like Melissa, Gail and Bette,
was studying voice): "I would see her there, and

she remembered me through Charlotte. She'd sit through part of my lesson and we'd talk. But she's a very private person and I'm a very private person, so it was never any kind of very social intercourse."

After Bette's spring tour in 1973, Robin ran into her again. Bette asked her when *Superstar* was closing and told her, "I'd like for you to come sing for me. I might need you this summer."

Robin recalls, "I sort of freaked out. I was very impressed. And three or four weeks later I got a call to go to Barry Manilow's house."

Apprehensive, because she had never seen the live act with the Harlettes, Robin went to the audition. "There were two other girls there. I later realized that she called sixty-five or seventy girls that week, and she would see them in groups of three. So I sang with these other two girls. Barry taught us a couple of the songs. I could read music so it wasn't too hard. He ran it down a couple of times, and we did it. One of them was 'You're out of the woods, You're out of the dark, You're out of the night,' from *Wizard of Oz*, which is very high. One of the things was, you had to be able to hit those notes to get the job. We also did 'Boogie Woogie Bugle Boy,' which I wasn't familiar with, but I could read fast.

"And then I left. Bette said, 'I'll call you,' and asked if I knew any other people. They called me back and asked me to come down on Sunday, to make the final decision. I was very nervous, because by then I'd figured out all these people were going to be there, people I thought had a lot of talent. So I went down again and sang with two completely different girls, that I'd never seen.

"And Bette said, 'Thank you. We'll call you tonight.' And I went home and my phone was out of order. I was a nervous wreck. But I had an answering service, so I kept running down to the public phone booth on the corner to see if there was a message. Finally there was, saying 'Call Barry Manilow.' I did, and Bette was there and said, 'I'd like for you to do the thing.' She said she was going to have Charlotte back again and 'a girl named Sharon Redd, another dark diva.' So I thought, Gee, I'm going to be the only white girl with these two black chicks? And I have no rhythm! This is going to be *very strange*!"

None of the other five women who have been Harlettes—or even Bette Midler herself—can hold a candle to Sharon Redd in terms of Performance Dues Paid. Sharon's varied career has taken her from the black honky-tonks of South Providence, Rhode Island, to a life of luxury, doing *Hair* and television specials in Australia; from radio and television jingles to a $700-a-week job doing back-up echoes for Petula Clark.

Born in Norfolk, Virginia, Sharon lived for a while in New York City, then followed a lover (a disc jockey), who promised to help her with her singing career, to Providence, Rhode Island. She ended up at the local YWCA, flat broke, and went to the Y's office manager and told her her story. The woman gave her a job as assistant bookkeeper.

Next, afraid she was "about to forget my purpose in coming here," Sharon went to the local Urban League and asked them "who did bookings, who handled music, who was *the* person in that town." They sent her to Carl Henry, a man who owned Providence's best-known black record store and who occasionally did some bookings in nearby Newport. He set Sharon up with an organist who'd just gotten out of jail ("he'd been on junk"), and they played, as Bette would put it, the pits.

"I'd work from nine to five at the Y, and then they'd pick me up at seven," Sharon says. "We'd go to the sleaziest clubs, I mean the sleaziest, tackiest clubs *in the world.* The black clubs in South Providence." (South Providence can give the worst areas of Harlem and Bedford-Stuyvesant a run for their money. Brown University students take their dates up on a hill near campus on summer nights to watch the abandoned tenements burn.)

"The stage was just about so big," Sharon continues. "And there they were, grabbing your ankle when you were onstage trying to sing. So there I was, and I said, 'I don't care. I'll pay any price because I want to sing,' I contended. I stayed there for two years."

Then came a phone call from the old lover, who had entered an old tape of Sharon's that he had in the Schaefer Talent Hunt. She won. "I got this long-distance phone call telling me that I'm the winner of the contest and that I'm going to get X amount of dollars and I'm going to do commer

cials and *all this*. So I came back to New York
and went right back to bookkeeping again. It was
so funny, I'd be sitting there, running this adding
machine, and I'd hear on the radio, 'And now
here's the red-hot sound of Sharon Redd,' and
this commercial would come on and I'd sit there
praying that the people I was working with
wouldn't hear it and fire me for not planning to
stay with the firm for a lifetime."

Through her stepfather ("all the men in my
family are in the business"), Sharon got onto
Channel 13's *Soul*, and started working with an
arranger who also happened to be musical director for *Hair*. He suggested she audition, and,
"Next thing I knew I was flying over the ocean,
twenty-four hours in the air, to this strange, white
country, Australia, to live for a certain amount of
time. It changed my whole life. I plan to write a
book about that, myself, someday. If I do become
successful in this business, I'd like to give black
children the opportunity to travel. Instead of
sending them to camp, send them *out*. To Europe.
Africa. Australia. Asia. So they'll know what's out
there for them, so they're not living a small existence. Small thinking. Small theater. Small movies. Small music. Expand the whole thing for
them. That's what I got, having lived in another
country."

After doing *Hair* for a year in Australia, Sharon
went off on her own there, singing in clubs, doing
commercials, even landing her own television special ("I was kind of the black Clairol girl"). The
producer who had brought her there to do *Hair*

wanted her to do another show; she refused. He went to the immigration department and reported her; they tried to deport her. Sharon's plight got picked up by the press, and she became a *cause célèbre*. "It got really super big. Newspapers, television, radio. Students from the university."

She won the immigration fight, but ended up returning to the United States anyway. Though she got into a show right away (the highly praised *Iphigenia* at the New York Shakespeare Festival Public Theatre, in which twelve actresses played twelve aspects of the Greek tragedy heroine's personality), she wasn't exactly pleased about being back in the United States: "I hated this country. I lived so well in Australia. I could be myself, I didn't have to go through any images, I didn't have to go through any politics about, well, they can't use this black person for this, or you're too light for that, or you're not dark enough. None of those head hassles. I could just go in and do a commercial there. It got to the point, in Australia, where I could just work on weekends. On Mondays through Thursdays, I'd just get a Bentley, with a driver, go pick up a lobster, head for the beach and just stay there all day. Come home, do whatever I had to do, and go back out at night. There was nobody to say, 'Who are you?' Or, 'What do you think about this?' Just none of this shit. I could really get into myself. I saw my first double rainbow over there, and I thought, 'This is it. I've never seen a double rainbow in America. I'm never going back to that dirty, polluted, political country again.' And here I am."

A couple of the other splits of Iphigenia's personality were doing studio work at the time, and suggested that Sharon do the same. Then one of the studio musicians informed her that Petula Clark was looking for three back-up singers: "Seven hundred bucks a week. And accommodations, food, everything is paid for." Sharon auditioned and got the job. "I got out there," she recalls, "and I was so depressed. Talk about a frustrated singer. Long black dresses. Standing way up in the back of a thirty-two-piece orchestra behind the cellos. Never to be seen except at the end of the show, when she says, 'And these are my angels.' Never to be introduced. No one could really see us. The light would go on, and off.

"And there we were in Las Vegas, where even the *daylight* is artificial. You never know what time of day it is. And Petula was nothing like Bette. She did not want to make contact with other female singers. It was like, you are my servants, you're working for me. Maybe at the end of the week, I'll take you out to dinner. Which will be very formal. No one's very relaxed. No one even wants to go. Since then, I hear she treats her singers much better now. They're even exposed."

Sharon tried out to be a Harlette while still with Petula. "I'd never heard Bette's music. I didn't know what she was into. I only listened to WBLS and the jazz stations. But everyone advised me to make the move, so I did, and it's one that has changed my whole life." Once accepted, she gave Petula a week's notice and plunged headlong into a new life style that at first confused and upset her, but eventually liberated her into a whole new image of herself. And the path that Sharon took to understanding Bette and relating to the madcap world in which she moves is significantly representative of the complex attitudes of hundreds and thousands of Midler fans across the country: straight or gay, young or old, hip or square, black or WASP, the one thing they all have received from Bette Midler is a sense of self, of being what they really *are* to the fullest and happiest degree possible.

Sharon was confronted with a life style peculiarly foreign to her upon becoming a Harlette. Her formative years had been spent in a totally black environment. ("Coming up in the South, I did not even talk to white people, because I was not around white people. Totally black schools, black church, black stores. Everything was a totally separate life.") Even in Las Vegas and Australia, she had chosen a rather sheltered, private life for herself.

Becoming a member of Bette's entourage, she was confronted with a life style that was very big-time New York, as well as one that was predominantly white and significantly gay.

"I had many gay friends, gay male friends," Sharon recalls. "But it hadn't become a part of my life. There was a whole slang which I did not understand. A whole way of living. A whole other language. And I just didn't *know*. I was on the defensive all the time. Every time somebody would say something to me, I thought, Oh, they're just tearing me down. I didn't understand that

that was just the way they were . . . That it wasn't *serious*. I had always been a very serious person."

One rehearsal in particular sticks out in Sharon's memory. "I was very quiet. I came in reading my little *Ebony* magazine, and everybody was making fun of me, saying what are you doing reading that shit. And I'd get very upset, just all the time. So André de Shields, who was our choreographer, André came in and said, 'You know, Sharon, I was just talking to someone about you from Australia.' And I said, 'Oh, really?' And I was very up about it. And he said, '*Yesssss.*' And he was looking me up and down, and his shoulders were moving, you know. And I said, 'What do you mean?' I really was getting uptight. And so he said, 'Never mind, *honey*. It's all *right*. They had a *lot* to say about you, though!' And I said, '*What* are you talking about?'

"And that's when Bette stepped in, and that's when I really started liking Bette, because I didn't know how to approach her either, up 'til then. I didn't know what she was about. I didn't know from nothing. I even thought maybe she was gay, too, at that time, though she isn't, of course.

"Anyway, so Bette says, 'André, *don't do that shit!*' She said, '*Tell* her. What's the matter with you? What kind of games are you playing with her?'

"And then everything was okay. She was saying exactly what I felt. But I didn't want to say anything, because I didn't know anyone and I didn't want to cause any friction, because it was at the beginning of rehearsals and I was going to be with these people for who knows how long. So I thought, Wow, she's really nice, because she had no need to stand up for me. And then everything started feeling comfortable.

"But I was always saying, 'What does that mean? What is that? What do you mean by that?' I simply knew nothing about 'the circuit.' "

The change did not come overnight, though, even with Bette's help. Once the group actually got out on the road, Sharon was still cautious, and the kind of outrageous audiences that Bette attracted gave her a further shock.

"I didn't know what to expect from the tour. So here we are, and we get there to the first place, in Maryland. And all these divas are in drag. Glitter, painted bodies. Quaaludes. Every possible drug. And I say, What is this? It was exciting, but I couldn't tell anyone how different this life was for me. 'Cause when I was working, it was strictly sequined tops and velvet skirts and lots of 'When Sunny Gets Blue.' That sort of thing. From there, to the little bitty things I was doing around New York, to Bette Midler. Which was an extreme for me. So here we are with all these insane people. But I'm really excited. I've like crossed the line of fear. That fear thing, I've gone beyond it. Because it's just too exciting for me to be uptight or nervous or anything like that.

"So the next day, a group of one of the Harlettes' friends came to see us, and I was approached in my room by both a male and a female that wanted me sexually. So again I thought, How am I gonna handle this? Because I don't want to be a total outsider to these things. I don't want people to say, 'She doesn't know what's going on.' And yet I didn't want them to think I knew too much that was going on either.

"But yet I had to exist in this existence, you know, when I was really a very simple kind of person. So head adjustments had to be made, and that was the biggest job for me. Not the music, Bette's music was good, but you weren't completely loose in what you did. Everything was set. Certain notes you sang, even though you could freely go beyond them, to a certain extent. But it wasn't like each man was a soloist backing up this person. So, that part I could handle all right.

"But it took an adjustment to a completely different type of people. Plus, I was a Southern girl, which is a whole other type of thing. Never having been around white people, because I came up during segregation. Sit-ins, boycotts, that whole thing. And not only were these people white, they were outrageous whites as well. Which was very exciting, and I loved it. And I'd gladly do it again, but of course, I'm a whole different person now.

"When I tell you one show changed my whole life, believe me."

One way that Sharon found of dealing with all the changes was to do what Bette advised all the Harlettes to try: create for themselves a character, some sort of combination of personal reality and fantasy, patterned similarly to her own alter ego, the Divine Miss M. As Sharon describes it: "Bette told me, the very first rehearsal, she said, 'Sharon, you gotta forget about Sharon Redd. When you're on that stage, Sharon Redd does not exist.' Like I said, I had not seen her act, and I didn't know what to expect. I had no idea that my thighs would be showing, that I'd be shaking ass all night and giving you lots of tit. So she told me that I'd have to forget about me, whoever that was, because she didn't know who or what I was either. So she said, 'Forget about you. You gotta find yourself an attitude. Whoever your favorite trashy person is, or whatever kind of person, get that character.'

"So I said, who do I know? I mean, all the black divas that I'd ever seen, their whole thing is just lots of *this*"—Sharon offers a big plastic smile and stretches her palms out high to the left and the right—"but I don't want to be just lots of *this*. I gotta go beyond that. So I said, Well, it's gonna be 'eat shit' from now on. I'd come right out there and my attitude toward them all would be 'eat shit,' all of you. And I would *not* crack a smile.

"So I went to a costume house, right? Still I didn't know, because all the groups I'd ever seen, they all wore lots of slink, giving you pretty pretty. 'I'm so pretty. I'm a pretty singer.' But not really giving you a character. So we go and get these costumes, and Bette's picking these things out with one arm, all cut way up here on the leg, and *really gaudy*. And I thought, Are we gonna wear this? And I thought, Oh well, so what, Sharon? If you're gonna do the job, you must go there. So we got these skirts, and my legs were showing, and I thought, My God I've got terrible legs. Just, ooooh, ooooh.

"Well, when I threw on that costume, I knew Sharon Redd was dead. I had to kill her every night. So I thought, What am I gonna be? All right, so it's gonna be 'eat shit,' but how do you get 'eat shit' across to an audience, who just see this group of people and don't know you, but you, Sharon, have to project something out there.

"So, I decided to use my head and my hips and just throw everything I've got right in their faces. And so the character came into form, along with the little hairdo that I had, which was very period. I had many little hairdos, and they all helped."

Charlotte's character was called Miss Crossfire, which had, in fact, been her nickname long before she became a Harlette. After a while, she had to tone down the character (just as Bette had to tone down Miss M): "That was another thing we had in common, Bette and I. There were two alter egos. I had to put Miss Crossfire to sleep, I had to like turn her into something else, to try to sedate her. That part of me was very talented and very alive, but it was also very poisonous and destructive." At times, Charlotte would get so deeply into character as the evil, dishy Miss Crossfire that it would be hours after she came offstage before she could come down.

Sharon, on the other hand, found her character a kind of protective device: "I liked doing it, because I still had myself when it was over. Because with my own act, I'd be out there and I'd be singing songs and I'd be pouring my guts out, and when the whole thing would be over, I couldn't even talk to anybody, because I was just *raw*. I'd exposed *me*, entirely."

Robin also had some problems initially with getting into character as a Harlette. "Bette used to talk a lot about character," she says. "She used to tell us right from the beginning, me especially, because I'm quiet and I'm fairly sedate, that we should be somebody else onstage, that we had to take it somewhere else. And it got to be easier after a while. But for me, it was very hard at first. It was just all very new to me, working in front of the number of people we worked in front of. Worrying about the singing, the choreography. The costumes helped. She'd always tell me, you've gotta be trashier, because I always looked kind of clean onstage. Charlotte is outrageous, of course, I realized that I couldn't compete with Charlotte or Sharon, because obviously I could never go to that place. Charlotte is crazy onstage, you know, just her own wonderful belligerent self. And Sharon just gives you lots of hips and lots of teeth. But Bette used to get on my back about being sleazier. At one point, at the beginning of the tour, she bought me a blond wig, thinking this would help. Luckily, I never had to wear it, because I put it on and I felt like an idiot, and I think she realized it wasn't quite the right direction either. But finally, about halfway through the tour, I really got into the character. And the character that I chose was a sleazy type of character, but almost a haughty sleaze. It wasn't, 'Well, you want some, guy?' It was more, you know, 'Well, if you want me, you can have me for a price. Or if I find you appealing.' That way, because I couldn't go the other way. I knew I could never compete with the other two girls that way. It was foolish to try. And I couldn't possibly compete with Bette, being the other white girl in the act. The only way to go was just to be sort of haughty and 'I-beg-your-pardon.' "

The result of the three alter egos (four actually, counting the Divine Miss M) working together onstage was extraordinary. Gail Kantor sums it up: "When Melissa, Merle and I did the thing, we really did not have it captured the way the other girls did. It was a much more subtle cheapness. Bette tried to bring it out more in us, but I think we were a little shyer. It was not because those girls were more willing to cheapen themselves than us. I think it was just because they were looser as performers, and more willing to get into it."

Moreover, Charlotte feels that Bette herself —her presence onstage with them—was vital to their being able to capture the attitude: "Bette could do it. Because the Harlettes have an attitude, with her. With somebody else we just sing. Like with Barry on his own tour. Though we were good, I think. We added a lot of spark, but we didn't really have an attitude onstage. We just stood there and sang. It was a lot different with Bette, and we were very, very conscious of attitude, of character. Bette told us to do this, this and this, and there was something that we picked up from being with her, something that was char-

The Palace, Act One.
The many faces of Bette
Midler in performance.
(Photos by Frank Teti)

The Palace, Act Two. Bette in her slinky sequined slit-skirt number. (Photo by Frank Teti)

acterized out of her own Divine Miss M persona.
She knew what she wanted and she gave it to us,
and it worked better with the three of us than it
worked with the other three, the first three girls.
They were a little slower. Then by the time I got
into the group, it had started to click. And when
the other two girls came in, it just completely
came together. Just like magic."

The new Harlettes rehearsed for six exhausting
weeks, working on the music with Barry in the
daytime and on choreography with André de
Shields at night. Robin speaks for all three in
calling it "the hardest rehearsing I've ever done in
my life." Bette also attended most of the rehearsals and always had the last say, on both the
music and the choreography.

Gail Kantor came in to some of the early music
rehearsals and helped Barry teach the new parts
to Sharon and Robin (Robin recalls it as being
especially helpful in terms of who sang what,
since Merle and Gail had sometimes switched
back and forth between "top" and "middle" voice
in the harmonies; Melissa and Charlotte had always taken "bottom").

"Barry's an excellent musician," says Robin,
whose father is in the music business himself (he
once recorded the Andrews Sisters). "One of the
finest I've ever worked with, and I've worked in
the studios of New York for a long time. He
knows his music and he teaches it well. It's odd,
because when I first saw him at the Baths, I
thought, He's sort of a quiet guy. And then he

sang, and he's a good singer, but he has no great personality, he doesn't try to be a great personality onstage. He doesn't have this 'Here I am, I'm gonna be a great star' attitude. But, I was impressed with his music, his teaching us the parts. He had everything written out, but the other two girls didn't read that much, so he ended up teaching them by ear. The new things that we did, like 'In the Mood,' he had recorded with Bette and he had written everything out for her. She did all the parts on the record herself, and there must be eight overdubs of her, and we had to do it bit by bit, because she doesn't read music that fast either. And when Barry taught it to us, he figured out which parts he was going to give to each one of us. He's a fascinating musician, because he knows exactly what he wants, and he knows how to teach it, which is fascinating, because some people know what they want and have no way of conveying it to other people who don't read music."

When Peter Dallas showed me around Bette's old apartment on West 75th Street (which he inherited when she moved down to Barrow Street in the Village), he indicated one spot at the side of the front room, saying: "This is where she worked. She used to do a wonderful thing over here. She would stand about two feet away from the wall and do her entire show in fast motion, which was amazing to watch. No mirror. She would just do it to the wall. She wouldn't sing it out loud. She'd just get all the movements down pat, before a show at the Baths. We'd just be sitting there talking, and she'd say, 'Give me a minute.' And she'd walk over here and she'd do the whole thing, real fast, and then she'd be back and say, 'All right, where were we?' "

Movement has always been an integral part of Bette's act. Even when she didn't have much stage space, as at Mister Kelly's in Chicago, the energy was constantly going. (Al Fullerton remembers that at Kelly's she did "a lot of bouncing up and down with the mike in her hand, and her head being thrust forward, a lot of tossing and turning kind of movements. It wasn't a lot of running and it wasn't a lot of campy gestures. It was a lot of energy, but it was all in a concentrated area. I think she was trying to let you know that she wanted to give you her all, but she didn't really have the room to scream and run. She used the stage as best she could, got all that there was to get out of that standstill energy.")

Michael Federal recalls: "She always moved, if the stage was big enough. That's the only difference now. She's got bigger stages. But, yeah, she'd be all over the stage. I never saw her as being conscious of specific movements as much as being conscious of moving, period. The idea of just getting around, like she had ants in her pants. She had to move. *Had* to."

Robin describes the process by which the Harlettes were given movement as follows: "Every number that we did was choreographed. Bette's own things weren't. We weren't choreographed with Bette; we were choreographed separately.

She was there almost all the time, though, when we were rehearsing. A lot of the things that we do, the little gestures and things, were her gestures. Some of it was brought from what the girls had done before, but it was all more elaborate with us and more set than the old choreography had been. Bette would watch us while André would run us through a few paces, things that he thought were good ideas, and she would watch, and she'd say, 'Well, I like the first two, but what about if we go to the left on the third one?' And she'd show him. And André would say, 'Yes, that's a good idea,' or, 'No, it won't work.' She was very aware of dance movement. And all the things that she does onstage, which sort of fit in with us at times, and other times she's completely by herself, were all her own things.

"She's good," Robin continued, describing Bette's abilities as a dancer. "I don't know how much she studied. She gets very frustrated if you can do something that she can't. And I'm not a great dancer, but she always wanted to learn. Like, Sharon is a fabulous rock dancer; she has certain things that she puts in. And Bette would always want her to teach her those things. She wants to know what's going on. She's very fast, she picks things up right away. But she wants to know what's going on and how to do it, to prove that she can. She's a good dancer, she does rather well in her own odd style, sort of a combination of rock-and-roll and modern, with leaps and hops and things. I get a kick out of watching her. She does different things every night, too. You never know quite what to expect."

André de Shields considers himself more Bette's "boogie master" than her choreographer. Born in Chicago, his educational and performing career has taken him to San Francisco; Philadelphia; Madison, Wisconsin, and Europe. He came to New York with the Chicago-based Organic Theatre Company's production of *Warp* (which only lasted one week, following vicious blasts from the New York critics) and decided to stay.

André met Bette when she came to see *Warp* back in Chicago during that madcap engagement at Kelly's in September 1972 (the Enter-Aaron-the-Baron sequence). "She loved *Warp*," he recalls, "and in turn asked me to come see her at Kelly's. Somehow, I learned that she was a great fan of potato salad. So I made potato salad for her. And brought it to her at Mister Kelly's, after the show, right to her dressing room."

Bette and André started talking, over the potato salad, about the act. "When I saw her, the Harlettes were simply great singers. They were moving, but there was no orchestration to their movement. And that was what Bette wanted, some sort of orchestration for the girls to use, to look as one. So I offered my services to her, just as a friend. I went to Kelly's and we worked for an afternoon and got some basic things together. I said to her, When *Warp* comes to New York at the end of the year, if you're still working with the Harlettes and you think you could use me, just give me a call."

The following January, André had moved to New York and was living with Charlotte Crossley, who had, coincidentally, just become a Harlette. He and Bette started talking business again, and when she started getting the tour together in late July, André became her boogie master: "I talked with Bette and I talked with Aaron, and I began working with the three ladies, all on the basis of what I knew they could do, and what I knew we could do together. I served as their boogie master. Didn't want to be their choreographer, because that scene connotes something of the likes of Peter Gennaro.

"It was easy," André continues, "because I was doing something I loved. I knew everybody involved, and everybody involved knew me. We knew each other's limitations. We knew just how far we could be stretched, how much we could do. So it was a matter of just going in and saying, 'Oh, yeah, that looks nice. Why don't the three of you do it?' I didn't really have to teach them anything. What they needed was a third eye. A person who wasn't specifically involved, who knew what was going on. So that you could separate the bad shit from the good shit."

André himself had never put together an act before, though he had staged some dance numbers for the Organic Theatre Company. He had also never formally studied dance: "I'm a street dancer. Everything I know comes from people I know, from situations I know. I have five brothers and five sisters. That's a whole galaxy of your own, a family like that. You're always picking up on other people's vibes, other people's attitudes, other people's dispositions. And you're always being put in the position where you have to adjust, adapt, flow with whatever vibrations other people are putting out."

So, André's process was to pick up on the vibes from the group itself, from Bette and the three Harlettes. His own research included getting to know Bette on the dance floor. "We were great dance partners for a while. At the *After Dark* Ruby Awards. In Chicago, we danced together too, and we've attended parties together and danced a lot. So by the time when I was doing the choreography for the Harlettes, I had a feeling not only of her attitude and showmanship, but even of her own *body*. I had *felt* her impulses when we were dancing together."

André feels that "ultimately Bette Midler was her own choreographer. She didn't have the time and she didn't have the perspective to sit out in the audience and say, 'Oh, that's wonderful,' because you can't talk to yourself that way. You can't sit in the audience and see yourself work onstage. So she needed somebody else."

But what went down definitely reflected the prime mover in the act, Bette herself. "First of all, Bette has an endless, an inexhaustible reservoir of energy. Even when she's just sitting in conversation, even when she's just eating lunch. You see the energy just jumping out of her. Not that she's a nervous individual. It's simply that one is always aware of a vitality. When she's performing onstage, there's never any need to control it. You

just give vent to all those energies. Just let it all
out, in every direction. Those things that escape
from her, in terms of dance energy, that I saw that
the three Harlettes could use I took and gave to
the Harlettes. Now it was a cycle. It was definitely
a cyclical thing. Bette would look at the Harlettes
and see herself. She just expanded on it. And
since it was her own shit anyway, there was never
the need to look out the corner of her eye and see
if they were still together. Because you know the
pattern was there, the design was there. And there
were times when, by accident, she wasn't doing
the same step. That didn't detract. It looked like a
kind of counterpoint.

"And all it took was just reminding her: 'Remember yesterday, when you did such and such?
Or 'Remember ten minutes ago when you did
such and such? Why don't you do it again?' And
she'd say, 'Oh, that's a good idea, André, I think I
will.' Or, 'You're full of shit, André, I won't do
that.' "

Bette also had a sense of her total body—that
movement could happen in any part: "This makes
choreography incredibly easier, when you can
take something that's happening in her head and
put it in her hips. Then you can go on forever,
and never be stymied, never be stagnant, never
reach a stalemate."

Everything about the movement was also related to that prime factor of the Midler mystique:
attitude. "We had to know how to truck, we had
to know how to Suzie Q, how to Charleston, how
to do all the dances that are now popular on *Soul*

Train. We also had to know how to be tasteful, how to be trashy. The important thing, even more than learning specific combinations, that the three ladies had to do together was attitude. It wasn't just steps. As a matter of fact, most of the time was concentrated on establishing the proper attitude. And I don't know whether this is any kind of phenomenon, or any new trend in the performance arts, but I don't run into many people who attack their craft from that standpoint. I've done a couple of other staging or choreography gigs since. And the concept with attitude is always something that you have to teach the people. What sensibilities are right. How to convey the proper posture. And once the attitude is established, once that is achieved, everything else is very easy . . .

"Bette's attitude, of course, was one of street lady. She spoke the language of someone you'd meet on the corner. She gave you the same kind of gesticulation, the same kind of body language of someone you'd meet on the street. And her ladies, her Harlettes, had to do the same thing. Long before the Harlettes were really trashy, the name Harlettes took on a kind of vengeance, a kind of deliberate offensive attitude, a kind of hard woman reputation, that the girls had to live up to. So because of that a lot of work was cut out for us. Much of the idea of working with attitudes is so subtle. It has to do with nuances. It had to do with whether you put your palm on your hip or your fist on your hip. Whether you're shaking your ass double time or whether you're shaking your ass quadruple time.

"A lot of the creating of the boogie that the ladies did came in actual rehearsal time. We'd go into a studio and we'd put on a tape and we'd just dance with each other. Bette was there for a lot of the times, and there were some times when we had established a direction for a particular song, or a particular moment in the show, that we were sure about, and that we knew could only get better and more complete, and she wouldn't bother to come in. She'd come in some other day when we had finished it, and she'd look at it.

"Sometimes I'd say, instead of just doing it by trial and error, 'Tell me what you'd like to see. Show me something that you love to do on the stage, and then let me enlarge it.' So she'd show me something that she did with her arm or with her hips or with her neck, and we'd fill it out.

"I think the best help that I got from Bette was that she's a good dancer herself. She lets music move her to do whatever she feels like doing, and that's the important element of creating dance. Not that you've really *studied* anything, that you've learned any specific technique. You just let your body go when the music moves you."

Broadway choreographer Michael Bennett was also called in to help with some of the period pieces, "Boogie Woogie Bugle Boy" and "In the Mood," in particular. "He was an expert," André says, "trained in styles. So after I did what little shit I could do with those two songs, he came in and polished it. I'm proud to say that he didn't have much polishing to do. A lot of my guess-work, from talking to my parents or watching old movies, was correct. A lot of the things that I stole from movies and records was authentic looking."

But most authentic looking of all were the boogies that André and Bette and the Harlettes gleaned from their own memory banks of everyday "popular" (in the "of the people" sense) dance: "I honestly believe, as corny as this sounds," André says, "that this is a rhythmic existence, that everybody's disposition can be interpreted in term of vibrations, of frequencies, of rhythms that shoot out, not only to the music that you hear on the radio, or the stereo. To the music of their living, of their lives. And being one of eleven children you've just got to know what space you can fill, at what times. When you've got to move out, when you've got to move in. When you've got to pick up the feet, when you've got to put them down.

"And that's exactly how I found Bette Midler. Not so much into a formal kind of dance, where you have to do this here and that there, but just whatever *happens*. If it's good, it will support itself, it will complete itself. If what you're doing in terms of dance is good, it will give you all the information, all the elements, that you need. All you have to do is figure out how the puzzle, how it's all going to fit together."

"The large fashion parade of homosexuals and other assorted oddities," wrote a snitty reporter from the *Washington Star-News*, "that made up half of the audience at a Kennedy Center appearance last spring was back Saturday night" (for the opening of Bette's tour at the Merriweather Post Pavilion in Columbia, Maryland), "but they constituted only about ten percent of this audience. The remainder were concertgoers who would look normal at any concert." Exactly how the reporter arrived at his figures is hard to say. Perhaps he went around making a head count, asking people if they were fairies or "normal concertgoers." At any rate, the grueling four-month tour that was to take Bette and her entourage to the Palace was underway, and it was to be, according to those concerned, a time of anything but normal concertgoing.

"We were really nervous and we had all these costumes and we were crazy and Bette was crazy," recalls Charlotte, who's known for speaking at times in a rather nonstop flow of consciousness, "but it was good for her to have us on the road, because she had some women to relate to, and this is the first time I ever worked for a woman before. I really learned a lot from her, because she's a great actress and she's a great singer and she's an incredible person, and I learned a lot about myself and I learned a lot about her, too, through that experience. We had a lot of really rough times on the road, but it really brought us all together. And we all became friends."

The pressures of the thirty-five-city tour were many, physical as well as mental. Sharon says, "I've seen Bette, in one town, when she was just hanging over the toilet, literally hanging over the toilet. And I thought, How is she gonna do it? How is she gonna get out there and perform? OK, onstage. And she was out there, click click click. And then she'd turn around to us and she'd go, 'I want to die,' in a very Tallulah Bankhead voice. And then, it would be *back* to the audience, and they'd *never know*. You know, *characters*, back and forth. It's very schizophrenic, but it helps you get through this business."

Robin remembers Bette having bronchitis once in Florida: "But she still gave them a hell of a show, and she came off the stage soaking. I never saw anyone work that hard. I mean, I might perspire a little, *tasteful* little bit, perhaps on the clee-*vage*, but she would be just drenched. Her hair would be just wringing wet."

Robin preferred the hectic three months on the road to doing the tour in pieces. "I think they felt they'd just like to get it over with in one fell swoop, instead of spacing it out. I think it's better in a way, too. I couldn't have done it if we were still doing it, in pieces. It was better to be out of town for three months at a time. It keeps the momentum going. You don't come home and forget about half the act and then have to pick up and go out again."

By the time they made it back to New York, everyone was feeling the strain: "We were all sick at the Palace. For some reason, after you've been on the road, and there's all that strain, when you get back home it's really hard to keep going. And there was something about those three weeks in December, with the worst weather we'd had in

New York, and Christmas coming up. Suddenly, I had the worst cold I ever had in my life, and Sharon was sick, too. And Charlotte pulled her leg out. And then I started thinking, I wish this would be over soon. It was hard to get through the Palace."

According to Charlotte, "Aaron wasn't around as much as he was the first tour. In fact, Bette was always trying to get him not to come, because she liked having the peace, the tranquillity, the good times that were in the group, like a karma that was very light, that wasn't heavy, that wasn't a lot of difficult anxiety trips to go through, a lot of possession trips to go through."

When Aaron was around, there would be arguments. "I'd walk into their dressing room," says Charlotte, "and all these things would be thrown around, after they'd fought and everything. So much tension around, you know. She'd have Bill Hennessy flown in to be with her. Bill was always a good factor in the group, because when he was around, or Bruce Vilanch was around, everybody was *up*. They'd come and talk to us, and we'd discuss things. They really took a lot of the edge off the tension that was going down. When Bill was around, it was much easier on us. Bette felt better, we felt better. Everything. It was real good."

Bruce Vilanch, who along with Bill Hennessy has been the chief contributor of comic material for the Divine Miss M, got to know Bette chiefly through her engagements at Mister Kelly's in Chicago, where he's an entertainment writer for the daily newspaper *Chicago Today*. Bruce and Bette, however, have very similar roots: they're both Jewish; their parents lived in Paterson, New Jersey (as mentioned earlier, Vilanch's father in fact once dated Bette's mother, when the two were still single); they both grew up as young loners in love with the entertainment industry. "We always joke that we're the same person," Bruce says. "She always tells me that I look exactly like her, without the beard. That when we were fourteen, we looked exactly alike."

Vilanch, who sports a figure somewhere between roly-poly and rotund, was an only child. "I grew up with a strong interest in theater," he says. "Broadway musicals. My father took me to see all the musicals, every single one of them. He bought me albums and librettos, so I would memorize everything. He had grown up in New York in the days when there wasn't television and all that. Just vaudeville. So that whole tradition was his. He always worked very hard, and he found the theater very relaxing.

"I was a very unhappy child," Bruce continues. "I was pretty wretched. I was fat and ugly and had no friends. I was only happy when I was at the theater or at the movies. Or watching TV or performing in front of the mirror.

"My parents went out a lot to clubs, too. And took me along. I was the only nine-year-old in New York with a charge account at the Blue Angel and the Bon Soir. I was *devoted* to Frances Faye at Basin Street. I used to go see her every night. And Kaye Ballard and Lenny Bruce at the Bon Soir. I saw Barbra Streisand when she was opening for Vaughn Meader at the Blue Angel. And I was there one night when she opened for Lynn Carter, the night of the Cuban missile crisis. She had been opening her show with 'Happy Days Are Here Again.' A big up-tempo version. And there everybody was, sitting watching the television at the bar. And Kennedy was announcing the end of the world. There was no question in anyone's mind that this was it. It was all over. Everyone sat there so incredibly gloomy, and she came on and started doing this song. In the middle of the first verse, she stopped and said, 'No, wait a minute. You're weeping. We really should do it the way it's happening.' And she just happened to have a new arrangement, that she had gotten the day before, the slow version, that's on the album. And she started doing that. It was absolutely heart-stopping. Incredible. No one had ever thought of it in that light before. It was absolutely wonderful."

After graduating from high school at the age of sixteen, Vilanch landed the role of Barnaby in the road company of *Hello, Dolly!*, which he played for a year. Then came college at Ohio State, where he majored in journalism and theater, with summer intern work on the *Miami Herald* and the *Detroit Free Press*. Then, *Boys in the Band*, both in New York and London ("I was the first fat Emory they'd had").

He then applied to some sixty newspapers for a job, and ended up at *Chicago Today* in June of

1970 ("the same day as Watergate, but two years ahead") and then the *Chicago Tribune*.

That same fall, Bette Midler made her debut at Kelly's, and she and Bruce actually became acquainted for the first time. "I had seen her in a few things back in New York," he says. "In *Miss Nefertiti Regrets* and *Fiddler*. But that was sort of coincidental. I didn't go because she was in them, though I recognized who she was. My mother had said, 'I think that's a Midler from Midler's Cleaners. They have some girl in their family and she's acting. They moved away from here years ago. They're really not from here any more.' "

Bruce actually began writing material for Bette in September 1972. When Bill Hennessy began to retreat in the wake of Aaron Russo, Bruce started to contribute more and more.

Hennessy and Vilanch had a very compatible relationship. Gail Kantor remembers them working closely together at the beginning: "Bill did a lot to help smooth over the transition." Hennessy respects Vilanch's material ("he's a good writer, a very funny man"), even though Bruce's humor was somewhat different than his own.

"My humor is more political than Bill's," says Bruce. "And mine is, I don't know, I used to think it was self-depreciating in a way. I suppose it is. But I'm much more line-y than he is. He was much more involved with the whole creation of Miss M. I really didn't come on as a force in the show until all that had been well founded.

"When I came on the scene, Bill and I discussed the character. We both felt that it had become too bitchy. I saw one concert when I first went on the road with her, and it was just an endless series of put-downs. When she finally came offstage, you'd say, 'Well who does she like?' Both Bill and I said to her, 'There has to be joyousness about it. We can't let it become that. All that stuff is too funny to let it become obsessive.' And she absolutely agreed.

"My principal love of the whole act is the parody of show business. I love the theater, and I tried to accentuate that. And at the Palace, where I was really doing most of the stuff, we brought in a lot of old show business things. Sophie Tucker and Sarah Bernhardt and Talullah. And a lot of those kinds of references, that sort of parody of show biz conventions.

"It's very interesting to see that Bette and Liza Minnelli are the two big ladies now. Because Liza embraces all those conventions. And she gets away with it. All that garbage like, 'Start by admitting—' and the house lights come up and the back stands up and the audience begins to get excited. That's all trash, just garbage. But she gets on, she loves it, she does it all.

"Of course, we do it, too. It's the same principle at work. But Bette does it differently. When everybody stands up and sings 'Chapel of Love,' it's not that they're being manipulated into doing it, it just happens. And although we make fun of that kind of thing, we ultimately wind up using it, too."

Manipulated or not, the audiences were generally wildly enthusiastic, and, more often than not, they were pretty outrageous as well (no matter what the *Washington Star-News* says). "I remember once," Robin says, "when we were in Virginia. I looked out at the audience, and I turned to Charlotte and said, 'You won't believe this, but the Tin Woodman, the Scarecrow, the Cowardly Lion and *Dorothy* are sitting out there, in the third row.' Naturally, during the 'Optimistic Voices' opening to the show's second act, the quartet went wild.

"Nothing really freaks me out," says Robin, "but that did. And the other time was Halloween night in Tampa, where we had a gentleman in *complete bridal ensemble*, with floor-length veil and hand bouquet, come in during the middle of the first act. It was a crazy night anyway, because Halloween in Tampa *is* crazy, plus tornado warnings were up, and it was one of those weird, wild, stormy evenings. And suddenly, in the middle of about the third song—no, Bette was doing some rap, and this guy just came *breezing* in, singing, waving his bouquet around. Every eye was on him, of course. Ours too. We couldn't believe it. He got to his seat and did a huge curtsy. He was obviously there for 'Chapel of Love,' because the minute we did it at the end, he was berserk, on top of his seat and everything."

Robin also recalls, "One night someone leaped up on the stage. I think it was in Chicago. Some gentleman dressed in long underwear and carrying a bugle, came streaking down the center aisle and leaped on the stage and grabbed Bette and planted a kiss on her. I got very apprehensive. We're supposed to have some sort of security. You don't know what people will do. He obviously only wanted to do that, but people are strange, you know, and that really shook her. Because he really grabbed her. I was ready to hit him with a chair. I didn't know, he could have had a knife or something. He might be crazy."

Similarly, during the Palace engagement, someone rushed the stage and Bette dived under Barry's grand piano. But, as Robin says, "Most of the time people were all right. There were a couple of times in concerts where the people got very close to the stage, several times at the Palace, in fact. People would press in close to the stage at the end and try to give her things. She was pretty good about that though. She'd stay just far enough away that nobody would try to grab her."

Sharon says, "One night they had to drag a female off. And many times, *many times*, there would be some child that just loved her so much that they had to touch her. They'd just jump up, and they'd have to carry the body right on off, screaming and kicking."

It was pretty much the same crowds everywhere," Charlotte says. "Everything from heavy, heavy drag queens to just a lot of really nice people. I remember Denver, Colorado, in particular. It was real mellow, real 1968. Those rocks. We were outside, and it was like, well, they're not man made. God had put them there. It was real back-to-nature, and it kind of flipped us all out.

"But every other place, there were heavy drugs in the audience. Heavy, heavy drugs. The first show we played at the Armadillo War Headquarters in Austin, Texas, was like the audience was right *there*, a few feet from us, and everybody was standing up, with their bottles of beer and Cutty Sark, joints being passed and passing joints to us up on the stage, and it freaked us out, because they were really, like rowdy. But Bette got control just like that" (a snap of the fingers). "When she really wanted to, she had, like a power, a force, that could really help her command attention. They were like fantastic the rest of the evening. It was fabulous. It frightened the shit out of me!

"And there were lots of other instances where these people would get into this amazing drag, flipped-out drag, and buy seats, like in the first row. You know, sit *orchestra* and just be outrageous. Like, when we were in Miami Beach, and all these little Jewish princes and princesses came out in the most unbelievable '50s cocktail party drags. I thought that was *fabulous*."

Still, after a while, as Charlotte says, it got "real boring, amazingly boring—everyone out in their drags, just fashion show to *death*!" Also, audiences that are very stoned are not always the most appreciative people to play to: "This last tour, there were a lot of people so stoned that they just sat there. I mean, we were kickin' ass onstage, and they were just goin' 'Duhhh.' And we would dish them from the stage, and they wouldn't even know it. And sometimes Bette would really *dish* them, you know. If you saw the show at the Pal-

ace, you know she was dishing people all the
time. Like the first night, the people who walked
in there, my dear, they were just 'I'm better than
you, so you entertain me.' And it was really heavy
karma, like walking into Reno Sweeney's on
talent night."

Not all the places they played were quite that
outrageous. "Actually," says Robin, "the places
that you think would be outrageous weren't, and
vice versa. Hollywood was quite conservative. Of
course, we played the Universal Amphitheater,
which was outdoors, and it was cold. People had
jackets and blankets. Maybe whatever weirdness
they were wearing was underneath that. But,
Phoenix, *Arizona*, which is a very conservative
area, had some of the most outrageously dressed
people I have seen in a long time." (Perhaps it's
simply a question of which cities needed Bette's
liberation most . . .)

"The thing that struck me so much," Robin
continues, "was the fact that Bette did attract such
a varied crowd. In almost every city, you had a
couple of very heavy drag queens, maybe one or
two, but not too many. And you had a gay following. But there were a lot of couples, young people
from, say their twenties to their late thirties, and
you had a surprising number of older people, with
gray hair.

"My father is in the record business, but he's
sixty years old. And he thought it was the best
show he had ever seen in his whole life. The best
live show. That's it, you know. Entertainment. It's
a show. She always gave the audience what they

paid for. I've been to the theater a lot in my life, and I've never seen anything worth a twelve-dollar ticket. But with Bette, I would say that no one ever went away disappointed. No matter how rotten she was, if we had a cold or we'd be down, she always gave them a hell of a show."

Audience reactions were almost always positive, but they did vary from place to place. Robin feels that Bette's style is very New York, and that certain audiences took longer to catch onto the rhythm than others: "The remarks she makes are fast, and she fires them out fast. In certain parts of the country, they don't catch on as fast as they do in New York. They're not used to hearing people speak fast. Especially in the South, laughs were slower in coming, which threw everyone off a little bit, but always by the end of the show the audience was on its feet. Once in a great while, you'd notice a couple of people leave, but in general the thousand other people who were there were always screaming. Maybe there'd be one little old couple. I could see the wheels clicking as they walked up the aisle, 'Well, I don't see what all the fuss is about.' But, mostly the people, even the older people, would really get into it, the audience participation at the end. I got a kick out of that. Seeing my mother, in Philadelphia, who is fifty-six years old and very conservative, standing up and clapping, not because of me, but because of the entertainment that was being presented onstage. That was just great."

After the shows, some of Bette's classier admirers would come backstage to pay their regards. "We got to meet a lot of people who really, really respect her," says Charlotte. "I was really moved, because I'd always wanted to meet all those divas, the TV and movie divas. Cher Bono, Lucille Ball, Joanne Worley. It was great. It was really good for my head, because they were just people. They get in there and they make their bucks, and make their sleazy deals, but they're still people.

"When we played the Dorothy Chandler Pavilion, it was a week before the Academy Awards, and I walked into Bette's dressing room. She said, 'Come in here and sit with me awhile,' and Warren Beatty walks in, and I *die*. He walks over to me, and I'm just dying. There I am in my ratty-tatty bluejeans. And there he is with Joni Mitchell, and Cher Bono is there, and David Bowie and Claudia Linnear are outside, giving a heavy rock attitude. I didn't particularly care for them, because they sat first row, center, orchestra, sat there, giving this heavy rock attitude. And I didn't like that, because if I had come to their show, no matter how bad they were, no matter how good, I would have been appreciative, because as an artist, I appreciate what other people are doing. And they were just very *cool*. And I walked off and I said to Bette, who was that black bitch in the front? And I said, 'They was givin' you *heavy diva*, too.' And Bette was hysterical and said, 'Charlo, are you gonna—?' And I said, 'Yeah, what? I'm not going to do anything to them.' And then when they got up to the room, I was very cool, but I just *checked* them out. The people in the front are the ones you can always see, and they're the ones we always dish."

Bette was always cordial with the fans that came backstage (the masses, of course, weren't allowed, but she was polite to the autograph-seekers at the stage door as well, according to the girls). One fan-artist meeting led to a blossoming friendship: "Cher was the one," Charlotte recalls. "Cher really loves Bette and really loves us. It turns out Cher was one of the Ronettes who never got onstage, but recorded with them. I think it was the Ronettes, or maybe the Chiffons. But it was heavy dish, and Cher was just dressed to kill, giving you blue bell-bottom denim pants with studs and butterfly appliqués, tons of turquoise, tan, looking gorgeous, casual gorgeous. And she really loved us. The second time she came to see us, we were at the Amphitheater and she was really real friendly. She's a Taurus just like me, and I went right there, right toward her."

"In Los Angeles," Robin says, "we shared a trailer with Bette. A big one, at Universal Amphitheater. There were a lot of people there backstage. The Andrews Sisters came back to see her. That was fabulous. My father used to record them, years ago, and they remembered him. I was very impressed that they remembered my dad. And they loved Bette. She was impressed, too. She *is* impressed by other people in show business, especially people she admires. She's never blasé about the success. It's always like, 'You came to see *me*?' It was very refreshing to see that, and I've seen it many times and I know it's not a put-on.

"She was very impressed to meet the Andrews Sisters. And Lucille Ball came backstage and Bette was *on the floor*. And Nina Simone came back one night. And Charlotte and Sharon especially, but Bette was just, I mean, she was so *touched*. And Nina's very quiet. She said, 'I just want to say'—pause—'that I really like you.' And Bette said, 'I've listened to your records so often,' and then she went on, and she knew everything Nina had ever done. Bette could always hold her own, with almost anybody in show business, even older, more experienced people like Lucille Ball. I mean, she, for some reason, has something to say to everyone. She knows so many facts, so many bits of information, especially about the business, that people find *her* interesting, also. They realize she's not just another dizzy broad. Who, you know, does crazy things onstage. That she's an intelligent person."

Candy Leigh, Bette's ex-press agent, also recalls: "Bette was very impressed with Lucille Ball's work as a comedienne. She was very excited when she met her, and Miss Ball autographed a color photo for her and sent it to her framed. Bette kept it prominently displayed in her living room on Barrow Street.

"Probably most important to her, though, was the work of Laurence Olivier. When we were preparing the *After Dark* Ruby Award party in Bette's honor—her first big award party—I told her she could invite anyone she wanted—that I, in fact, would make the invitations out for her to anyone she wanted. Her only choice was Laurence Olivier. He was out of town at the time. Subsequently, he did attend a performance of hers at the Amphitheater in Los Angeles and was, apparently, wild for her. He gave them a wonderful quote which they continued to use in their ads for some time. I know she was very touched."

Following the show, there were occasional dinners with local producers ("If someone was giving a dinner, we all went," Charlotte says, "Bette always demanded that we go out with her then"). Otherwise, Bette very seldom went out after a show, to parties or bar-hopping with other members of the entourage. Robin describes her as, "A great late movie buff. And we always would get together in somebody's room and watch *In Concert* or *Midnight Special* on television, and usually ended up throwing things at the television, because we hated who was on, and we would just dish them to pieces. And throw things at the screen."

One of the few parties Bette did attend was one in Albuquerque, New Mexico. "It was a birthday party or something," Sharon recalls, "and Bette went. I was really shocked that she was gonna go, because she didn't go out. We got there and who greets us at the door, but this person whose face is sprayed gold, his hair is gold, his outfit's gold. He's gold from head to toe. And I go, 'Oh, no, not another one of these.' *Many* dykes. *And* straight people. It was a totally mixed party. Very freaked out. So I found a chair in one corner, because I definitely did *not* want to talk. I'd gotten to the point on the tour where we'd done over half of it. I was just tired of the same questions, the same everything. So I just sat in the corner and watched, and she just partied with everybody. Everybody was surrounding her, and she was dancing with everybody, just giving it to them, just like out there onstage, you know. Dancing with the gold-sprayed man, I looked at her and I just didn't know. This whole thing was like very frightening. Because I just didn't know, well, what is it? And she went *right there*. But it was one of the few times. Most of the times we just went out to dinner, with promoters and things, which bored the shit out of me. I couldn't see how she did that, which I would never do. They would *kill* me! But in one town, there were a couple of promoters who were really nice. They treated us exceptionally well. So we would go out with them. But other places—"

In San Francisco, Bill Graham gave a party for Bette at Winterland. The band and the girls arrived in the city earlier than Bette, and headed for the party. "So we all went ahead," says Charlotte, "and when we get to the door, they wouldn't let us in. So Bette gets into town, and she goes there and she says, 'Are my people here?' And they say, 'No, they came, but we turned them away.' And she left too. That was her whole trip: If my people can't come with me, then I won't come. If you can't treat them like you treat me, with just as much respect and honor, then I don't need you. Bill Graham ended up sending us flowers and

Bette, Charlotte, Sharon, and Robin in their slinky-slip line-up. (Photos by Frank Teti)

Bette and Sharon work out at the Palace. (Photo by Frank Teti)

being extra nice to us at the gig. He's really a sweetheart. It wasn't really his fault. It was just that heavy, *very* San Francisco bullshit, you know?"

In Chicago, Charlotte's parents gave a party for the group. "It was just my mother and father, my aunt and my Uncle Joe, and my cousin, and everybody out of our band and friends, and Bette. It was the greatest. Bette came, and my mother made the most incredible soul food dinner. We really had a great time, and that's when Bette really got to know me. She said, 'Now I know why you are the way you are.' She got really emotional and cried and said, 'Oh, your parents are so wonderful.'"

The tour also included Honolulu, and Bette threw a party at the group's hotel and her parents attended. "They're really nice people," Charlotte says, "but I detect a bit of sadness. Bette doesn't talk about them very much. Her mother is really very charming. And she's got a sister, Suzie, who is gorgeous, I mean *gorgeous*, really incredible looking. I like them all very much."

Often after the show, Sharon and Charlotte and some of the men in the entourage would hit the local gay bars. "Normally, on the road, after a show," Sharon says, "you're so up, your adrenalin is so, you just can't sit down and watch a movie, so most of the time we'd go out to a bar, usually a gay bar. I know every gay bar in this country, I think. Every one. I don't even need those guidebooks, you know. I can tell you what street, whether it's men and women, or all men, and what colors. You know, incredible. We'd go there, and we'd walk in and we were back onstage again, because all the queens would scream. 'Oh, dahling, you were so wonderful. Oh, my dearrrrrrrr.' All you had to do was just stand there and slowly come down off your trip."

"The sad thing," Charlotte says, "is that the bars were all the same. Every gay bar across the country. They were full of the same types. And that made me very sad. It was depressing, because a lot of those people, well, Bette Midler is a lot of those people's *whole lives*, and when we played Tulsa, Oklahoma, you know, or some of those places, a lot of people had nothing else to do with their lives except be a Bette Midler fan, or a David Bowie fan. But they really went all out, and they were really nice to us. They gave us all the drugs we wanted, offered to help us do anything we wanted to do. Of course, Bette didn't go. Bette only went once, I think, and the place went wild. But they felt that if they met us, they had met somebody that was *with* Bette Midler, you know. And I found that very sad and depressing, so I ended up going to these bars and getting amazingly drunk, you know. Drinking for free and dancing and having a really great time."

Bette and the girls were together a good deal during their nonperforming hours. "A lot of performers never really speak to their group singers," says Robin. "But with Bette, we were always with her. When we flew, she sat with one of us. After the show, if she felt like doing anything, if we went to it, it was always with someone from the group. Or if we all got together in someone's room and watched television, or played cards. There were always lots of laughs during that time we were together. Very rarely did you feel like she was the boss, that you were working for her. It was like you were working with her. If someone had a problem, it would eventually come out. If someone was lonely, or had a problem with their old man or their old lady, the group sort of helped each other out in that respect. I think the most fun times we had were when we were just sort of sitting around. Laughing, dishing people in show business. It was fun to hear her laugh. She would just get hysterical sometimes and fall on the floor. That was her favorite thing. She'd get hysterical, and you'd look and she'd be on the floor, laughing and rolling around."

The four women would go shopping together (Charlotte recalls a department store spree in Atlanta, Georgia, where she and Sharon got some peculiar stares: "They must have thought we were her bodyguards or something"). Robin recalls Bette particularly liked to look for jewelry ("gold earrings, especially"), and also that she "just likes to go along and see what you're going to buy."

The four of them usually wore bluejeans, T-shirts, and leotard tops, Robin says. "And Corkease shoes, for us, and Spring-o-lators for Bette, which was a very stunning ensemble in airports. We really looked strange in places like Albuquerque."

Bette did not like being recognized, according to Robin, but was always polite when she was. "In general, when we'd travel, she'd always wear dark glasses, and her hair would either be set or up under a kerchief. But when people did recognize her, she was okay. She signed things, autographs. But she always looked a little uncomfortable, and I felt uncomfortable to be with her at those moments. She was never rude, though, never, and I've seen people be very rude. But she was always a little apprehensive, like, suddenly they had intruded on her privacy. Like, we'd be shopping or walking around and laughing, and it would make her very quiet for a couple of minutes."

To avoid recognition, the girls would call Bette a pet name. "One day she was depressed at the beginning of the tour," says Robin. "Out of the clear blue, she said, 'I wish somebody would call me Delores,' I don't know why. Just out of the clear blue. So we started calling her Delores. And the bracelet she gave us after the tour, the little ID bracelet, says 'Thank you, Delores' on it. And if we were in an airport or a public place, where people would know if we called her name, we would call 'Delores, Delores.' We couldn't yell 'Bette, Bette,' people would turn and look, because it's such an individual name. So we'd call, 'Delores.' "

Things got more difficult, however, with the passage of time, for Bette and the three other women as well. "I don't know," says Robin. "It just seemed like one long airplane trip after a while. I stopped counting at about fifty flights."

Charlotte, who is Buddhist, says, "My practice on the road was very difficult to maintain. Because there were all these elements around us. Some were evil, some were good, some were kind of, like, in the middle of the road, and they always had you going up and down, which really made, you know, for a lot of dependence on drugs. When I was in *Hair*, I used to depend on grass and everything, but for different reasons. For Bette's thing, it was different, not so much from being depressed, or bored, but because of the pressure. It was something to keep me from flipping out, because we were always on the verge of flipping out. We really had no home for those three months we were on the road. And even when we got here in New York, things were still zip zip zip all the time, you know.

"But Bette really took care of us. It was the most fulfilling job I've ever had, because not only did it encompass music and nostalgia, but there was a bit of theatrics in there, too. And we, the three of us, Robin and Sharon and I, are all actresses in a way, me more than them, maybe. But it was so good, because Bette was constantly giving us something, and giving it to the audience. The three of us had this incredible thing onstage. It was the most fulfilling thing. I'd love to work for her again.

"It was draining, of course. I found that I was so totally into being a Harlette onstage that it took me hours to come down. I'd go to those bars and those people would expect me to be a Harlette, and have that same kind of crazy energy, and I couldn't, you know, I just couldn't. When Bette's tour was over, it took me, like a month to cool out. Then I had to go home and visit my parents for Christmas, which was good, but it took me a really long time. Like, I was on a train that was going twelve thousand miles an hour. Just couldn't cool out, and God knows what Bette must have been going through. I didn't have any voice or anything by the time we were through. It was, like, the momentum was so fast, we were traveling all the time. Permanent jet lag. It took me a while to get over that."

6. repetition ad infinitum

the decanonization of the divine

Midler's career went into a serious slump after the Palace. For over a year she did not perform at all. Her accompanist and musical director, Barry Manilow, left to pursue his own musical career. Aaron Russo turned down project after project for her, and Bette herself more or less dropped out of sight.

In March of 1975, Midler and the Harlettes returned to Broadway in the lavish *Clams on the Half-Shell Revue*, directed by Joe Layton and featuring Lionel Hampton, at the Minskoff Theater. The show was successful, but most of Midler's old fans saw through the tinsel and stage effects (including a *King Kong* sequence) and lamented the fact that there was nothing new in the routines and that, sadder yet, Midler's voice was in worse and worse shape.

Three more albums followed, plus two more whistle-stop tours and some television appearances, and the feeling of we've-seen-this-all-before grew, even among Midler's most die-hard fans. As Midler repeated herself, picking up more and more of straight Middle America along the way, she began to lose most of her old trend-setting original supporters.

Many people who were close to Midler during this period feel that losing Barry Manilow at this stage of her career was a bigger blow than Bette herself has ever been willing to admit. Patrick Cochrane, who was Midler's private secretary for four months after the *Songs for the New Depression* tour in early 1977, says: "Barry was all those classic early-Midler songs. She's never done one since that wasn't a remake of one of his arrangements. When she lost Barry, she lost her confidence, because she never trusted anybody else to put the whole thing together like she trusted him."

Not that things were exactly hunky-dory between Midler and Manilow, as Bette herself admitted to writer Craig Zadan for his *New York* magazine piece prior to her Minskoff comeback: "Barry and I worked so fast. It was two ambitious Jews in one room. Such bitchiness. We would bitch at each other all the time. He very rarely did an arrangement I didn't like. He's a much better musician than I. We would mostly bicker about which song should go where and how the show should be paced—and whether he was going to wear white or not—and would he *pleeeeese* stop waving his head—and would he *not* sit on phone books, if he didn't mind—and could he get the bass player to stop tossing his blond locks about. He would always want to know how come I was always half a tone under and why I didn't come in on time, and it's true that sometimes he would insist on something that I would take to heart and get real spiteful about.''

Manilow himself told Zadan: "Bette and I hated each other in the beginning. It was a case of two strong egos clashing. But we knew we were good for each other, I guess.'' Occasionally Bette would change selections in the middle of a set, which infuriated Barry more than anything.

The fighting didn't bother Bette, though, who, for all the reports of her offstage shyness and quietness (she would have the press believe that she's a regular little bookworm), is equally famous for her frequent blow-ups with Russo, Manilow, her band and back-up singers, and her long-time press-agent Candy Leigh. "I like fighting," Bette told Zadan, sounding a bit like Italian director Lina Wertmuller, the bane of New York feminists —"I always thought that a woman fighting was very sexy. My sister and I would always fight night and day.''

Why had Midler waited so long to do the Mins-koff show? Rumors were rampant, but Midler told Zadan: "Where was I? I was sitting around getting very chubby for a year. But I was having the time of my life. I was bruised and battered and I needed a rest. So I went to Paris, France, to become very elegant elegant and I failed mi-ser-a-bly. You know, I thought I spoke French. Then I got there and I realized I didn't. But I ate my brains out."

She told Stan Mieses of New York's *Daily News*: "I needed a respite from the drive. After a while you get worn out. I'm not going to compare Garbo, but I think she made the right decision."

At any rate, with the Minskoff she was back, certainly as energetic as ever. The show ran ten weeks and grossed a reported $1.8 million.

Charlotte Crossley insists that Bette didn't much like the superextravaganza that Layton devised. According to the most outspoken of Harlettes, Bette resisted the overtheatricalized show from the beginning and never liked it, even though it was more or less a popular and critical success:

"What you had was a Broadway show, with a Broadway director, a person who for the most part did television and Broadway shows and is a brilliant, brilliant director. Joe Layton. Who directed Miss Strei-sand on TV and stuff. So this man *knows* what he is going after. So what happened was that we'd come into rehearsal and Joe would show us something and we girls would get it down pat, and then Bette would come in and she'd criticize it. All of us had come from the theater. But Bette had, too, and you'd think that her discipline of having been on Broadway in *Fiddler* would be such that she'd be able to relate

and make the transition from having done concerts to putting her head in a different place:
We're doing Broadway now. It's a certain attitude
you have to have. And she had a big aversion to
it. To that discipline. She didn't have that attitude. It upset her and she was constantly rebelling
against it, and I found that very unprofessional in
a way. And Aaron was the same. When a person
is not of the theater, does not have greasepaint in
his blood, he'd better be cool. And Aaron didn't
trust any of those people who were putting together the show, and they were all professionals,
they knew what they were doing, having done it
all before. I remember once, in a tryout in Philadelphia, Aaron threw an absolute fit. I was just so
embarrassed."

Shortly after the Minskoff, Bette also parted
company with another mainstay of her career,
Candy Leigh, who had handled her "public relations" since early 1973, when Ahmet Ertegun of
Atlantic Records had recommended her to Russo.
Leigh's job was never easy, for Bette seems to
have resisted her virtually every step of the way:

"Bette was never fond of participating in publicity," Candy says with circumspect understatement. "She disliked interviews and was appalled
at how often she was misquoted and misrepre-
sented. She also was loath to reveal anything
about her private life—which the press, of course,
was most interested to know. For all those reasons, I worked most often with and through

Aaron. Therefore, you could describe my professional relationship with Bette as 'distant.' "

Candy left the Midler camp—and also stopped doing press for Manilow, her other major client —directly following the Minskoff. "I had decided that owning and running a public relations agency was far too consuming. I wanted a long rest and more of a personal life." (Candy later went into personal management with Bette's former back-up singers; she reactivated her PR agency, Tomorrow Today, in early 1979.)

When Aaron asked her what he was going to do about finding a new press agent for Bette, Candy is reputed to have told him to "try an ad in *The New York Times* under 'Masochist,' " insisting that she'd had her fill of egos for a while.

In November of the same year (1975), Ula Hedwig, a young singer and actress from Chicago who had done *Hair* there with Michael Federal and Charlotte Crossley, got a call from a singer friend named David Lasley with the news that Bette Midler was auditioning for new Harlettes in New York. Ula (born Ursula) had just cracked a rib in the Toledo, Ohio, version of *Godspell*, but she caught the next plane, auditioned by singing "Wedding Bell Blues," and got the job. Rehearsals started the next day, with Ula replacing Robin Grean.

By this time, portraying a Harlette onstage had become almost as established and "set" as Bette's own presentation of the Divine Miss M. Ula had little trouble picking up what she was supposed to do, though she had never seen the Harlettes perform and had seen Bette herself only once, back at Mister Kelly's in Chicago, before she had the back-up singers.

"Actually, the other two girls filled me in on what to do rather quickly," Ula recalls. "Bette herself didn't say too much. Her two key words are 'attitude' and 'position, girls.' I was just told to be as *out* as you possibly can. Never too little make-up. Just pack the make-up on."

Ula's character was, however, considerably different from Robin's. "I don't see myself as any sort of vamp or glamorous image, so that's what I decided to go after. And when I put on that Frederick's of Hollywood dress, I immediately felt like a dumb blonde. That's what I tried to portray myself as—cute, dumb, and always off the beat. Very sleazy. I remember Bette coming into the dressing room and saying, 'Be more snooty, like you're smelling shit.' And I didn't want to do that, because I guess that was Robin's old thing."

During what was called the New Depression tour (named after Bette's *Songs for the New Depression* album), the "girls" were given a certain amount of leeway to add their own touches to the show, Ula says. "We did sometimes improvise onstage. As we went along on the road, we would have quips that we'd do back to her, and sometimes we'd keep them in the show. Sometimes we'd overdo it, and she'd turn around and glare at us. One time I blacked in a tooth in the front, and every time she'd turn around I'd close my mouth. I knew she wouldn't get off on it at all. The band

cracked up, though, and the people in the front
rows that saw it. When the curtain came down,
she ran up to me and said, 'Don't ever do that
again. It's just *too cheese.*' "

The Depression act started out with Midler in a
hospital bed (she had just had an appendectomy
before the tour) and featured a section with her as
a plastic lounge singer named Vickie Eydie; for
this, the Harlettes became her clones once more,
the Eydettes.

The show never made it to New York City but
played for a week up the river at the Westchester
Premiere Theater in Tarrytown. After four
months on the road, it looked tired and hack-
neyed.

After one more date, in Las Vegas (Bette's only
appearance there except for the time with Johnny
Carson in 1972), the act was put to rest for what
both Bette and the Harlettes assumed would be
the last time.

Following this came the second major hiatus in
Midler's career. From March, 1976, until late
1977, when she broke down and once more
started to Scotch-tape her old act together for yet
another cross-country tour, Midler did not perform at all except for some television and a benefit for gay rights at the Hollywood Bowl.

During this time span, Midler moved to Los
Angeles, and the Harlettes began to put together
their own act, shedding their old onstage characters layer by layer as they sought to establish their

own audience, just as former Harlette Melissa Manchester—and Barry Manilow—had.

A major conflict developed between the girls and their old nemesis, Aaron Russo, over the use of the name "Harlettes." As Charlotte described it, mincing no words (as usual): "We were performing at this club in Los Angeles, and they were so horrible to us there. They were very discriminatory towards women and black people. And straight people. It was just such nonsense. It must have been our second or third night there, and Aaron Russo showed up, and he came to raise hell. I still think it was against Bette's wishes. But our manager, Candy Leigh, had left town, and there he was. This motherfucker comes back to our dressing room and starts screaming, 'You girls are stealing, you girls are blah-blah-blah.' And I was ready to murder him. And nobody else said anything, so I dealt with him. I said, 'How much fuckin' money do you want for this goddamn name?' Then I said, 'Bette doesn't know you're here causing all this confusion, does she?' We finally got rid of him, because I said we had a show to do. And I went home that night and I had to pray for forgiveness, because I was so angry that if I'd had a gun, I would have shot him dead. I would have shot him fuckin' dead."

Charlotte continues: "So we got on the phone to Bette and raised all kind of hell with her. 'Who the fuck does he think he is coming in here telling us that? Did you send him over?' And she says, 'No, I didn't send him over there. Why did he do that?' Then she got on his ass. So we finally had to make an agreement with him that we would use 'Formerly of the Harlettes' for identification purposes only."

"Yes," adds Ula, "in parentheses, half the size of our own names. All these stipulations. It was absurd." Aaron also insisted that they add the word "of," so that they were formerly *of* the Harlettes, not (presumably) the whole (however past-tense) thing.

During this same time period, cable television's Home Box Office was showing a Bette Midler *Standing Room Only* show that Ula, Charlotte, and Sharon were not too happy about.

"We were told it was a reference tape for Bette's private use," Ula says. "I guess that's why we only got paid $160 each for it."

The HBO show nonetheless was such a success with the public that Aaron was finally able to get Bette her first network special, NBC's *Old Red Hair Is Back*, which aired December 4, 1977. Sharon joined Bette on the special, along with former Harlettes Robin Grean and Merle Miller. The show was relatively raunchy for prime-time national television ("Please try to remain vertical, girls, at least until the first commercial."), but the censors did snip a few routines, like the line about the Harlettes having "FDS-ed themselves into a stupor" before the show.

The special featured Dustin Hoffman and clown Emmett Kelly; it was generally well received, though the critic of the proper *New York Times* did accuse Midler of "dabbling rather heavily in sentimentality" in her ballad selections.

Asked at the time by writer Gerrit Henry if she foresaw doing more television, Midler replied: "A future on TV? Who's want a future on TV? Television is a medium that eats you alive. You can't keep turning out good material week after week."

Sharon recalls her being relatively at ease with the medium, however: "A lot of it was filmed with live audiences, with the stage built out so that she'd feel at home. Television is so different from rehearsing for a show—you can't just throw numbers in and out, because orchestrations have been done. It's all set. Costumes have been built, everything is timed to the T. There were a few incidents that they had. I remember she wanted Aaron to stay out of it. Ron Field, the director, cooled her out a lot. He had been around and had done a lot of specials. So he was able to relax her a lot."

The airing of the special coincided with Bette's late 1977–early 1978 tour, which she asked Ula, Sharon, and Charlotte to join her for. The three had also just done two special appearances with Bette, the CBS *Rolling Stone* Tenth Anniversary Special on television, and the ill-fated "Night for Rights" rally for gays at the Hollywood Bowl, where Richard Pryor had been booed off the stage for his reverse-racist antihomosexual remarks to the crowd. Midler had been scheduled to appear immediately after Pryor, and Sharon recalls that they were all a nervous wreck after the peculiar chain of events: "Bette was completely freaked out. After all that tension, we had to come out in green Ku Klux Klan robes, pulling her as the Statue of Liberty with a noose around her neck. It had a certain amount of comic relief, but Bette was freaked—we all were."

The Harlettes agreed to back Midler on the Copa tour in late 1977 only on the condition that they be allowed to open with their own act as well —not as the Harlettes, but as themselves: Redd, Hedwig, and Crossley. "We had been planning a tour opening for a big name," Sharon smiles. "We didn't think it would be *that* name particularly. But after Aaron made the offer, we thought it would be a good move, would let her fans and our fans know that we had a record out, at very little expense to ourselves. But it was expensive in its own way."

So the feud with Aaron was once again forgotten, and the girls were on the road again. Charlotte recalls, "Bette was very proud of us. Very supportive. But she was constantly dissatisfied with what she was doing. There wasn't much that she could say to us, because our shit was pretty tight. But, backing her up, we were rehearsing all the time, and it got to be horrible. It was just like beating a dead horse. There were certain things that would work, but others that just wouldn't."

What had initially been billed as "An Intimate Evening with Bette Midler" turned out to be not much different from what Midler had been up to for the past five years.

"See, what happened," says Sharon, "is that we learned a new show, and after that had been rehearsed and choreographed and everything, then fear set in. 'Maybe we should do some of the old stuff.' You know. 'Maybe we should leave it the way it was.' Or, 'Let's try out the new stuff.' We'd work on it, then, 'Oh, that's too difficult. Let's cut that out. We're working too hard.' We'd end up cutting steps out of numbers, and eventually the whole number would be dropped because everybody was scared because we never really put it on its feet properly. A lot of it sort of ended up being the same show by the time we reached New York."

Little by little, the new, "intimate" show had turned into the same old camp. The show wasn't different at all. "No," says Charlotte firmly. "It was the same old fuckin' show. Same *old*, *fucking* show."

"There were no sets this time," Ula adds. "There had always been definite sets before. This time it was completely loose."

"And the jokes were the same," Charlotte continues. "The drags were the same. The only thing that was different about the show was us, when we came out and opened for her. And our shit was very together. Aaron Russo couldn't fuck with us, because we would come into rehearsals and our stuff would be tight. The band would play our stuff, and our stuff would be down, and then we'd be there all day for her. *All day*. Her changing her mind. She couldn't make up her mind about anything. That was my only negative, and I let her know about it. I said, 'You waste too much motherfuckin' time. You always start at the last minute. You can't ever plan your shit.' And we were very used to our stuff going well. We had more control over what we were doing. Even if we weren't sure, it seemed like, between the three of us, we could come up with some kind of decision. It wasn't easy on us either, but we were nowhere as disorganized as she was."

The results were more than apparent at the Copa, where the show looked so disheveled and directionless that it was embarrassing. Furthermore, the producers (Russo and Ron Delsener) had crowded what looked like at least twice as many people as the room would hold inside, causing real fire-panic concern among many of the fans. Intimate indeed.

Charlotte recalls the long train ride to Cleveland, where the final performances had been scheduled, immediately following the Copa engagement: "So we were all on this train. And Aaron Russo was the most obnoxious person in the world on this train ride. He was walking up and down, stuffing his face full of Mr. Goodbars and O. Henrys. And was just so obnoxious. And Bette's movie people were on the train, too, so they were going over her *Rose* script. The whole thing was just real strange."

No sooner had they arrived in Cleveland than a tremendous snowstorm hit, and the first two days of performances were called off. That first night, the band and singers were hanging out in the bar at the Holiday Inn, where they were staying just outside Cleveland, enjoying the snowstorm, drinking and getting stoned. They decided to perform for the people in the lounge, an audience that, as

Ula recalls, "amounted to about five drunken businessmen and the people from the kitchen."

The band jammed first, then "Charlotte got up and did some cocktail numbers," Ula got "carried bodily up to the stage" and performed, Sharon sang, and at last Bette herself got up on the bar and let go.

"She finally got up at the last minute," Charlotte recalls. "She got up and we did—well, we ended up doing part of our show with her, and she didn't want to leave. Everyone was finished singing, and she just sat there. Sittin' up on that little bar stage, and all the band hung with her. Everybody just stayed. Everybody got very drunk and stoned. And she loved it."

Ula adds: "It was really funny to walk back into the lounge after going to my room to make a telephone call, and to see Sharon and Charlotte sitting there in the background, and there was Bette Midler, with this ski cap pulled over her head, no make-up on, leggings. Doing her schtick. Like, she was improving, and she was really grooving on it. It was terrific."

After two days of canceled concerts, the performances resumed. "The mayor of Cleveland came," Ula remembers. "He gave Bette the key to the city."

"Yeah," says Charlotte. "That was just before Cleveland went broke."

"Bette kept calling him Dennis the Menace," Ula adds. "The mayor. He's this little short guy. But he ended up giving her a police escort to the airport."

"Yes," Sharon adds, with a faraway look. "The mayor came and took Bette off, because she had to make this flight. Everyone else was taking the train again, because Aaron had heard there was going to be another blizzard. But the mayor came in his motorcade and we barely had time to say goodbye. And that has stayed with me a long time. Bette just said, 'Well, I guess this is it.' And that was the last time I talked to her since, or had any kind of contact. And I worked with her for five years. 'Well, I guess this is it.' "

7. approach to material

idols and incarnations

"I had a lot of things to say," Bette told Chris Chase in an interview for *The New York Times*, "so I had to find vehicles to say them. I did research. I'd find words which would call up images, colors, textures, what the room sounded like, the rustle of bamboo in the wind. I would find these wonderful songs, and that's the way I've been doing for years and years, trying to tell the stories, to fit in the textures."

Bette Midler's greatest talent is her approach to material. She usually chooses her songs with care, and the songs she does pick—and keep—she makes extraordinarily her own, rummaging around inside the words, pushing the original melodies out of shape and discovering, in the process, new meanings, new nuances, new directions.

In discussing his portrait art, Richard Amsel (the painter who did the covers for both of Bette's first two albums) told Henry Edwards of *After Dark*, "I'm interested in uncovering realtionships between the past and present and discovering how things have changed and grown." He could just as easily have been speaking for Bette herself about her own method of finding and working with material. She, too, looks for links between past and present, ferrets meanings out of flow and change.

"I guess I just have an affinity for those old ladies, the ones that did the torch songs," Bette told me in an interview just prior to her first date at Mister Kelly's in October 1970. "Mostly it's still dues to the roots—ragtime and all." And at that time, it was. "Mainly, I like going back to the beginnings, you know, Ma Rainey, Bessie Smith, Billie Holiday, Dinah Washington, Ruth Etting, Helen Morgan. Helen Morgan in particular. She was a brilliant actress and a brilliant singer."

Bette's affinity for the good old girls also extended to the actresses of the period. It's hard not to think of Joan Crawford in *Rain* as soon as you see the Midler tropical-frizz hairdo. Mae West, Bette said to May Okun of *The New York Daily News*, is, "a genius. She was renegade, she was bold and she had such courage of her convictions. Such a life she led and she wouldn't let anybody tell her not to. She just didn't care. She just stood up to all of them. She had her fantasy and made the world accept it." (When Okun noticed biographies of Lillian Hellman, Lillian Gish, Isadora Duncan and Dorothy Parker at Bette's apartment during an interview, she asked Bette about them and got the following reply: "I'm trying to figure out how they lived their lives and if there is anything I can learn from their lives that I can apply to mine.")

Still, the really strong identification was with singers, both past and present. Bette's favorites are almost all women (she admitted liking Joe Cocker, Otis Redding, Bobby "Blue" Bland, and Ray Charles to Dick Leitsch of *Gay*, but prefaced it by saying, "I don't have any male favorites because male singers don't really show it to you like the women do"), and they are mostly singers that one would term emotional stylists. When we spoke, she mentioned Nina Simone, Morgana King, Roberta Flack, Sheila Jordan, Judy Henske, Laura Nyro, Joni Mitchell, Janis Joplin, and Tina Turner—quite a range of styles, though *style* is, consistently, of prime significance to all of them. Phrasing, nuance, experimentation.

Bette's antennae were constantly out, looking for material she could use. "I consider that *work*," Bette said to May Okun. "When I go to the theater or movies or listen to a piece of music, I'm not doing it to enjoy myself. I'm trying to see what other people are into and how they're getting along."

Michael Federal recalls that when he and Bette were living together, "She was always on the go. Always doing something. She's very fiery, very fiery. Always likes to be going places." Her record-listening habits at that time (1971-72) had

moved on from the old torch singers she had
favored at the beginning: "I think she was pretty
well done with listening to the '30s and '40s stuff
by then. I guess we used to listen to soul tunes
mostly. I remember a favorite album of hers was
the one Laura Nyro did with Labelle, *Gonna Take
a Miracle*. And recently, she's crazy about the new
Maggie Bell album. She *loves* that."

On the road, Bette, her girls and her band
members all had cassette tape recorders. "They
were these *large* cassettes with stereo earphones,"
Robin recalls. "No one spoke to each other, ever,
on the planes. We'd just sit down, turn our cassettes on and listen. Bette listened to a lot of R &
B, current R & B like the Spinners and the Dra-
matics. And then we would switch tapes. Some
people were into jazz. I was into Mott the Hoople.
No one ever wanted to borrow my tapes."

Charlotte remembers, "We'd listen to music out
on the road and she'd always say, 'How does he
do that? How does that go?' And I'd sing it for
her. She was always very, very open in listening to
music. Very into gospel. And the Spinners. Aretha. We listened to a lot of that, mellow black R
& B, that funk-and-discotheque sound."

Bette's rock-and-roll roots occasionally came to
the fore as well. "There were times on the road, at
sound checks and things," says Robin, "where she
would get restless and start singing a lot of old
rock-and-roll. A lot of early '50s things that she
grew up on. And she'd want us sometimes to sing
with her, and we'd fool around and fake the parts.
I remember she liked all the songs from when I

was in about the sixth or seventh grade. 'Mr. Lee'
and 'Lollipop' and all the Chordettes kind of
thing, that had nice harmony. She liked things
that had harmony parts to them. All that shooby-
doo stuff from the '50s. She'd go into 'Lollipop'
and expect us to join right in."

Michael would bring music to Bette's attention
and found her open, but very selective about what
she really liked. "I tried to make suggestions
about what she should do and everything," he
said. "But the best thing is just to listen to what
you like. If something appeals to her, she'll go
after it. You can't really sell her on anything. She
had very specific things she wanted to do, and the
tune really had to appeal to something that was
deep inside her. It had to say something to her, so
that she could turn around and say it to other
people. She was very selective about what she
picked."

Bette was also rather vocal about what she liked
and didn't like, even though her choices might not
be currently "fashionable" (Bette certainly has
never been accused of being a trend-follower).
She told Cynthia Spector of *Zoo World*, "I always
loved popular music—popular things are prime
movers"—and went on to list not the Beatles and
the Stones, but Jo Stafford, Patti Page, and Teresa
Brewer. (Her love of "pop," however, evidently
did not extend to Burt Bacharach. Asked what she
thought of him by Neil Appelbaum in *After Dark*,
she replied: "I don't think about Burt Bacharach.
Ever! To me that's Muzak. Music has to pick you
up and throw you down again.")

Bette's search for material was a mushrooming process. Robin mentions the large stacks of sheet music on the floor of Bette's apartment, and the great number of record albums. "She's almost academic about it," Bill Hennessy says. "She would go to libraries, she would watch, she would talk to people. And she has the ears *of life*. She can *listen*. And she's very hard on everything, you know. I mean, she'd listen to, like, a hundred and fifty songs and she'd maybe only like one of them. Or listen to a hundred or two hundred jokes and only get one or two, and use those and just do the shit out of them."

Billy Cunningham, Bette's first accompanist at the Baths, used to argue with her frequently over material, but he thought her approach to some of the songs he did approve of extraordinary:

"Bette would take a song like 'Remember My Forgotten Man,' " Billy recalls. "Which was a depressing song. In the context of *Golddiggers*, it was a depressing moment. Here's a song that absolutely personified what was going on in the United States at that moment that the movie was made, the mid-'30s, that whole montage of men standing in bread lines. On the sheet music, you see men facing in opposite dirrections, on each tier of a rainbow. But when the lights came up in the movie, you could see that they were not really soldiers, they were men carrying spades and shovels, and some carrying crutches and what-not. The first few times I heard Bette sing it, I didn't know all that and I didn't *hear* it, because she didn't hear it. But the more she sang it, the more she

Bette emerges in *Clams on the Half Shell*. (Photo by Frank Teti)

King Kong takes Bette in hand in *Clams on the Half Shell*. (Photo by Frank Teti)

Bette in concert at the Roxy in Hollywood, December, 1977.
(Photo by Robert Scott)

heard it and the more I heard it, because it changed. And the more we did it, the more the audiences heard it. And would respond to it. Because that song doesn't make any sense out of context at all. I used to think her forgotten man was some guy she was in love with that she had forgotten about. Until I really began to listen. And then I thought, Oh, my God, it's like a Dalton Trumbo screenplay. It's rank with message. How did it ever get past the Hays office?" ("Remember My Forgotten Man" is one of the songs Bette discovered at the Lincoln Center Library for the Performing Arts: "It was on an old record there. I listened to it because it sounded like such a great title.")

Billy also recalls, "Bette didn't like 'Superstar' at first. I said, 'Think about it. It's nine-thirty in the morning, and you're up in your house. And it's *him* on the radio. And you had waited all day out in the cold, in the rain, waiting, and for somebody who singled you out and took you home. Fucked you within an inch of your life. And disappeared from your life. And your life won't stop. It has to keep going. Your life will continue to go on. You hear this, and you *remember*. And then you put on the coffee and wake up your husband and change the baby's diaper. And your life goes on. But for that one brief moment, you remember.' " Bette could listen to advice like that. And remember, herself.

"Bette pretty much inspired a lot of new modes of communication," says Gail Kantor, "because

singers who do not write can only express themselves well by means of the material they pick.
And if they're into expressing themselves, they're
not doing the big-time nightclub circuit, you
know, the Waldorf and all. So, Bette had developed a kind of ear for what she wanted to do
onstage. And the concept, even though she picked
so many different kinds of material, from different eras, had a consistency. In what she said and
what she did onstage."

In translating that material, Gail thinks Barry
Manilow was an important factor. "Barry understood it so well. I don't think she ever realized
how alert he was to what she did. I mean when he
came in, she had charts and things, for various
songs, from before he started working with her,
but he understood right away what she was doing.
He saw what was happening onstage without
being in the audience. And he was able to arrange
accordingly. And work with her on the songs, on
the concepts of each song, accordingly."

Both Michael and Gail recall that the early
arrangements (both vocal and instrumental) were
a kind of collaborative affair by all involved,
though Barry and Bette always made the final
decisions on what to keep. "And usually," Gail
says, "Barry had worked on the songs with Bette
before he brought them to us. So they each had
an idea of what they wanted. Other producers,"
Gail said, "are sometimes a lot less specific than
Barry was. A lot of studio work today is sort of
collaborative, as far as backup vocals go. The
producer has a concept in mind—you know, what

he wants us to sing—but the phrasing, the harmonics and the voicings, the back-up people come up with that themselves. Too many producers take singers for granted. They do the same thing with musicians. Very little is written out."

Bette's material, onstage and on record, does not fall easily into categories, for Bette is an eclectic in her stylistic approach as she is in her selection of material. And groupings, such as the following analysis, based on her performance selections up to the Palace, are therefore necessarily tentative, and many songs could fit into two or three different lists. (For example, almost everything that Bette is doing presently has some sort of rhythm-'n'-blues touch to it. The "folk-based" material never sounds like straight folk. And, in a very real sense, every song that Bette does is a "theater piece.")

Early Camp: Bette's Mae West number, "Come Up and See Me Sometime" (also recorded by Sophie Tucker and Ethel Waters, not to mention Paul Whiteman); her Carmen Miranda dress-up numbers, "Cuanta la Gusta" (done by Carmen and the Andrews Sisters in *Date with Judy*) and "Marijuana" (which Bette once said to an interviewer was from Earl Carroll's *Murder at the Vanities*, 1934); her Dorothy Lamour number, "Moon of Manakoora" (Tony Martin and Vaughn Monroe also recorded that one); Les Elgart's big-band piece "The Continental"; and Marlene Dietrich's "Hot Voodoo" number from *Blonde Venus*.

Genuine Nostalgia: "Remember My Forgotten

Man" from Busby Berkeley's *Golddiggers of 1933,*
"Bill Bailey," Lena Horne's "Good for Nothing
Joe," Bessie Smith's "Empty Bed Blues," and all
the Andrews Sisters songs: "Boogie Woogie Bugle
Boy," "Lullaby of Broadway," "Chattanooga
Choo Choo," and Glenn Miller's "In the Mood."

"50s Rock-n'-Roll: "Sh-Boom" (The Crew
Cuts), "Tutti-Frutti" (Little Richard), "Teenager
in Love" (Frankie Lymon and the Teenagers, or
Gale Storm, if you prefer—I doubt that Bette did),
"Shake, Rattle and Roll" (Bill Haley and the
Comets), "Great Balls of Fire" (Jerry Lee Lewis),
"Chapel of Love" (The Dixie Cups), "Uptown"
(not the Roy Orbison version), "Da Doo Run
Run" (The Belmonts), "Leader of the Pack" (The
Shangri Las) and "Do You Want to Dance"
(Bobby Freeman).

Rock: "Lady Madonna" (The Beatles), "Honky
Tonk Woman" (The Rolling Stones), "Daytime
Hustler," "Down on Me" (Janis Joplin), "Delta
Dawn," "Friends" (Buzzy Linhart), "Fat Stuff"
(Ed Holstein), "Breakin' Up Somebody's Home,"
and "See Me, Feel Me" (from *Tommy*).

Rhythm-'n'-Blues: "Could It Be I Stayed Away
Too Long" (Jackson Five), "C.C. Rider" (Chuck
Willis, LaVerne Baker and many more), "Higher
and Higher (Your Love Keeps Liftin' Me)"
(Jackie Wilson, Ike and Tina Turner).

Folk-based Material: "What Have They Done
to the Rain?" (Joan Baez), "Been on a Train"
(Laura Nyro), Joni Mitchell's "For Free" and
"The River."

Ballads: "Am I Blue" (Ethel Waters), Rodgers

and Hart's "Little Girl Blue," "That Lucky Old Sun" (Frank Sinatra, Sarah Vaughan and others), Leon Russell's "Superstar," and two Johnny Mercer tunes, "Drinkin' Again" (from Aretha Franklin's *Unforgettable* album) and "Skylark" (recorded by some of the best in the business, including Helen Forrest, Anita O'Day and Aretha).

Theater Pieces: Kurt Weill's "Pirate Jenny" and "Surabaya Johnny," and John Prine's "Hello in There."

Bette's first album for Atlantic, *The Divine Miss M*, was a long time in the making. Michael recalls: "We went in and tried to do it as a session thing. Eventually, we got a small audience, to try to turn her on, to turn the whole thing on. We did a couple of cuts with her and the whole band working at once, with a small audience on the side that she could play to. And that worked very well.

"But then she got into this ridiculous thing that her voice was nowhere. After hearing it for the first time on good tape machines. She got into this thing that the voice was nowhere and that she had to work on her voice. That she had to hold notes forever. I think she got a little too conscious of it. She got freaked out about it. Hearing herself. That's one reason it took a long time."

Another reason was that Bette did not get along that well with the album's original producer, Joel Dorn. "At first there was a little tension in the air, right at the top," says Michael. "And that didn't make it any more fun. It was a personality thing. Joel's very strong in what he wants, and Bette is too. And at the point, she didn't know exactly what she wanted to hear on the record, but she was pretty sure she wasn't getting what she wanted. And it upset her. And she would, you know, fight."

It ended up with Dorn producing five cuts on the album, and a team of three other persons (Barry Manilow, Atlantic president Ahmet Ertegun, and Geoffrey Haslam) being listed as co-producers of the other six cuts. For all the problems, however, the album got rave reviews, such as *Cash Box's* "Newcomer Pick" selection: "Oh, the wait! But oh, the record! It may have taken four producers and even more arrangers to translate her live excitement into recording excellence, but it has been done. And how it's been done! Lookin' for your next superstar, boys? Well step right up . . . Don't resist the tendency toward the superlative, it's bigger than the both of us."

The chief problem is that all of Midler's albums are schizophrenic. All are carefully geared to include "something for everyone." No one must be offended. And as a result, no one gets a really strong, clear picture of what's being offered.

Bette told one interviewer that her first album was going to be called *Out to Lunch*, which seems to indicate that it was centered around a concept, of camp, of outrageousness. The second was supposed to be "all bar songs." Had either of those albums actually appeared, it seems that they might have had an identity that albums with catch-all titles, like *The Divine Miss M* and *Bette Midler*, did not.

Without question, the Midler personality is multi-faceted; her musical interests are many and varied. But this does not mean that the time she spends in the recording studio can't be more channeled, that there can't be more of an indication of concept and direction in what she releases for posterity. Versatility in an artist is something that emerges naturally, that is apparent *in toto*, not something achieved by obvious selections of "contrasting" material.

In pieces, there are many things on all the albums that come off quite well. It's simply the adding up that becomes problematic. The parts themselves are rather good, even when they're more promising than fulfilled.

The old rockers on the first album ("Do You Want to Dance?," "Chapel of Love" and "Leader of the Pack") are tight, predictable, good-clean fun, just like the originals. And you want to hear them about as many times as you heard the originals. Like, four times a day for about a week. After that there's nothing to go back to.

The contemporary rockers fare a lot better. "Daytime Hustler" probably should have been Bette's first single, but the image-makers had something else in mind. It's straightforward and funky, and it has just enough rhythmic subtlety and vocal phrasing to keep you listening after that first week. "Delta Dawn" is a classic, showing Bette at her most eclectic best, borrowing the ache and slide from country singers without becoming hillbillyish or maudlin, combining the mellow country flavor with just the right mix of R & B rock.

The first version of "Friends" is a mess, full of cutesy overdubbing and the kind of vocal mugging that Bette can bring off delightfully onstage, but which falls completely flat here. The second version (the song is used to open and close one side of the album), on the other hand, works beautifully, delineating perfectly the lonely lady/outrageous clown dichotomy of the Midler mystique with its slow/sad opening followed by funky phrasing and rollicking rhythms. (Midler is an incredibly rhythmic singer; she knows how to get to the heart of a song and push it out of shape, playing around with it, syncopating against the given style, bouncing her voice off the instrumental or back-up vocal accompaniment, first blending, then contrasting the two elements. Perhaps Barry is to be thanked for some of this in his arrangements, but usually you feel that it's just *there*, innate in Bette's voice itself. You *feel* the voice relating to the environment around it, and that's the mark of a truly special talent.)

The closing of the second "Friends," in fact, exhibits on record the very quality that Billy Cunningham objected to about Bette in person—her predilection for improvising, for punching into the prescribed rhythms and phrasing, for doing the song not "the way it should be," but new. I still think it's Bette's greatest talent, and in the first album it is best exemplified, here and in the finale to "Delta Dawn," where, during the big build toward the climax, Bette literally lets the back-up girls take over the solo line and pushes against them with her own brand of funky counterpoint.

"Boogie Woogie Bugle Boy," with Bette playing all three Andrews Sisters (thanks to overdubbing) is the finest example on the first album of her ability to treat nostalgic material with both respect and a touch of spoof. The attitude is slightly different than the attitude toward the '50s rock-'n'-roll numbers (Bette, after all, grew up with the latter, not with the Andrews Sisters), and that extra inch of distance adds an extra edge of interest. (The album version of "Boogie Woogie Bugle Boy" has it all over the re-recorded single in every respect: the harmonies are more sophisticated, the horn sections are stronger, the piano boogies better, the rhythmic interest is far greater. Barry Manilow told *Rolling Stone* that his version (the single) was faster, with "punched up horns," and that the album version, by Joel Dorn, had "an old-fashioned effect, not in tight three-part harmony." He went on to say, "The differences between mine and Joel's is that his is really authentic and mine is bright. I didn't go after the authentic part, maybe because I didn't know how to do it, and it probably wouldn't have come off good on television anyway." He first worked out the arrangement for Bette on a Burt Bacharach television special.)

Not surprisingly (considering the fact that studio gimmickry and overproduction probably have ruined more good music in the past fifteen years than all other negative factors about the recording industry combined), some of the best moments on both albums feature the very simplest of arrangements, usually just Bette singing, with Barry on piano. Even "Delta Dawn" is established this way, with the guitar and back-up vocals (still soft and mellow) not coming in until the second verse. The contrast of the build at the end is thus set up, and is therefore a good deal more effective.

"Hello in There," the good version of "Friends," "Superstar," and "Am I Blue" all start out with piano alone as well. The arrangement for the John Prine song poses an interesting irony between mood and message: While the lyrics speak of aging, loneliness, war and death, the piano (Pat Rebillot on this particular cut) tinkles almost merrily and the strings (arranged by William Fisher) gush. Again, the subtlety of the contrast is extraordinary. (Dorn is responsible for this cut and for "Am I Blue," and it would be interesting to see what *he* could do with a whole Midler-concept album, too.)

"Am I Blue" is the ultimate woman-left-lonely song, which Bette picked up from Ethel Waters, whose careful "throwaway" style contemporary listeners probably don't know as well as they should. Bette learned much about understatement and subtlety of phrasing from singers like Waters and Billie Holiday. The arrangement on "Am I Blue" is again beautifully simple, tinkling piano (Manilow), straightforward rhythm bass, whisk drums, and just a hint of acoustic guitar.

"Superstar" has never been among my favorite Midler numbers. It sometimes works pretty well in person, but it doesn't merit five minutes and nine seconds on the album.

The two opening bands of Bette's second album, "Skylark" and "Drinking Again," are so much the best things she's ever done on record that everything else unfortunately suffers by comparison. Curiously enough, they are also among the few numbers in the Midler repertory that come off better on record than in person.

"Skylark," a Hoagy Carmichael tune, with lyrics by Johnny Mercer, was a staple of the Big Band era, when the vocalists were kept carefully subservient to the boys in the band. Helen Forrest recorded it with Harry James; Anita O'Day, with Gene Krupa. Forrest's version is an interesting study in warm controlled understatement. O'Day takes some nice liberties with the vocal line. But neither gets much of a chance to do much more than fill in after the long instrumental introduction, and neither gets to *sing* the finale.

When Aretha Franklin recorded "Skylark" on her *Laughing on the Outside* album in 1963, the record industry's focus had changed considerably. Though hardly one of Franklin's stylistic triumphs (it's arranged and conducted by Robert Mersey, probably the most ineffectual—at least in terms of capturing Aretha's particular talent for vocal styling—producer that she's ever worked with) the soft meaningfulness that Aretha does find in the lyrics points nicely toward what Bette was to achieve with the same material ten years làter (minus the schlock arrangements, the studio-strings "sweetening," and the overlushness of the vocal itself in the Franklin version).

Bette's "Skylark" pits her beautifully against only one instrument: Barry Manilow's piano. A very special interplay develops, with the voice's achieving not just a flowing lyricism, but a distinct identity, a kind of forthright *characterization* as well. Bette becomes someone who is singing about herself. Making herself, or a part of herself, the subject matter of her song. When she sings the line about "sad as a gypsy serenading the moon," she's suddenly very Jewish, very New York City, very much the funny lady of her act. Yet there's nothing really campy or superficial about the way she delivers the line. It's just that it indicates something, some underlying part of her that's not being specifically stated out loud. What we're seeing is not so much Miss M showing through in a serious song by Bette Midler as that *part* of Bette Midler out of which Miss M grew. A kind of strange combination of reality and fantasy. Which may be why the song is such a knockout.

Another Mercer song, "Drinking Again" (with music by Doris Tauber), likewise probably came to Bette's attention thanks to Aretha, since it is on the *Unforgettable* album, which Ben Gillespie introduced Bette to and which she maintains had such an impact on her. (Though Mersey again produced that Aretha album, this is one of the cuts which, according to Leonard Feather's liner notes, "were made with the assistance of a small and sympathetic accompanying group for which Mersey supplied minimal written guidance.")

Aretha's version, this time, is quite a stunner. She begins the song with the kind of soulful wail that has become her trademark—and the feeling never stops (it's exactly this kind of wailing feeling that is missing from her "Skylark" interpretation). Bette's version is distinctly her own, with character again proving a major factor. Using a kind of honeyed rasp, with a bit of country "catch" thrown into the voice, she achieves the same kind of intensity that Aretha gets out of her wail. Substituting "a bottle of beer" for Aretha's "bottle of Seagram's" at the end (different life styles?), Bette goes on to a hushed and simple climax, nothing at all like the elaborate sax, organ, and voice build in Aretha's finale. Again, Bette and Barry have gone it alone on this cut, and it's beautiful.

Side One of the second album continues with Denise LaSalle's "Breakin' Up Somebody's Home," a nicely tongue-in-cheek liberated-lady song. I'm not wholly satisfied with the drum-heavy, R & B brass-blast arrangement, but Bette's vocal is excellent, showing, with a very different type of material, the same sense of style and nuance that she established on the Mercer cuts. She sounds a lot like Genya Ravan (former vocalist with Ten-Wheel Drive) here—a decidedly complimentary comparison, for Ravan is probably the best (and most seriously underrated) woman rock singer we've had to date except Joplin.

"Surabaya Johnny," the Brecht-Weill song from *Happy End*, follows on the album, but pretty much misses the mark (it was better at the Pal-

ace). The song demands a very cool, presenta-
tional style. The album version pushes too hard,
gets a bit over-emotional in spots, and, ironically,
loses its real dramatic contrast by trying too hard
to be "dramatic." Barry does a nice job with the
piano accompaniment, but the rest of the arrangement gets a bit syrupy as it goes along.

"I Shall Be Released" is, along with the two
Mercer songs and "Delta Dawn," really essential
Midler. It takes only a bar or two of the bass-and-
piano fluid, open-ended introduction to make it
evident that this is special stuff, and from there on
out things just get looser and better. Bette plays
around with the melody line and with the lyrics
(both of which are rather extraordinary to begin
with), making them even more personal, more
crammed with a peculiar kind of simple-yet-sub-
tle meaningfulness.

Other than Bette's, my most distinct memory of
this Dylan/Band song (perhaps the most significant song written in the past ten years) was a very
different version by folk singers Jim and Jean in
Chicago during the Democratic National Convention in 1968. Real days of rage and repression,
defeat and disillusionment. At the end of their act
(it was at a club called the Quiet Knight) they
started slowly into "They say everything can be
replaced—" in a haunting arrangement, woven a-
round the sounds from an acoustic guitar and tiny
finger cymbals. Suddenly, it was as if the lyrics
really meant what they said—that, in spite of
everything that was going down at Daley's circus

down by the Stockyards, something, somehow, still could be salvaged.

Bette's version came five years later, when, if anything, people were even angrier and more disillusioned. And a lot of that anger and waiting comes out in the way Bette sings the words. The message of hope remains, but there's nothing sad or soft about it any more. No more pie in the sky. Liberation is yours for the taking, she seems to insist, building the "any day now" promise into a powerful, repetition-crescendo, improvising new words as she goes. "Any day now, I shall be free again. Any day now, my life shall be again." Vocally and lyrically, Bette has turned a classic song of quiet resignation into the ultimate cry of liberation—for gays, for women, for whoever needs it. Any day, now.

As good as Side One of the second album is, Side Two is problematic. The songs seem all to have been picked more to repeat past successes —to retread familiar paths—than to show what Bette can really do best or to take her into new territories. "Lullaby of Broadway" lets her camp it up as Mae West. "In the Mood" brings out the three Andrews Sisters—Patti, Maxene, and the late Laverne—for another go-around, proving (again?) that "Miss M sings all vocal parts," that thanks to studio gimmickry she can be a whole trio (or even more). "Uptown," "Da Doo Run Run" and "Higher and Higher (Your Love Keeps Lifting Me)" repeat the formulas perfected with the soul-and-oldies approach of "Chapel of Love"/ "Leader of the Pack"-type material on the first album, with only "Uptown" (which I really rather like) maintaining much interest in its own right (again Bette's characterization, of a woman who gives her man self-respect, is superb).

I do like some of the things Bette achieves vocally. Her Big Band sound on "In the Mood" *is* damn good, done as it is with such a quietly cooled-out kind of control. Similarly, she uses an intentionally "not-big" voice in "Uptown." And there's even something fascinating about the way she sharps and flats the vocal line of "Twisted" completely out of shape, though her on-the-whole cutesy approach doesn't particularly do justice to the Lambert-Hendricks-Ross number.

The finale of "Higher and Higher" is also interesting, with the back-up girls doing a kind of double-time, rhythmic drive-to-climax, while Bette herself comes along slow and high, softly singing around inside the framework that the girls establish. Such creative harmonizing is one of Bette's most effective vocal abilities, and here it serves to whet your appetite to flip the second album over and get back to the really good stuff—"Skylark" through "Released."

Eliot Hubbard, publicity director of Reno Sweeney (New York City's youth-oriented night-club-cabaret) and a friend of Bette, had invited her over to his apartment for brunch following her run at the Palace. Out of politeness, he had stashed the new *Rolling Stone* (predated January 17, 1974) away where she wouldn't see it, thinking that if she hadn't seen Jon Landau's vicious re-

view of her second album that it would be just as
well not to spoil their meal. As luck would have it,
however, someone else had left a second copy of
the paper around, and Bette went right to it.

Despite my own personal reservations about
parts of the second album, Landau's broadside
can only be considered a snide and devastating
personal attack. Though in the very same issue
Bette is picked as one of the two Rock Stars of the
Year (with the following citation: "In 1973, Bette
Midler did her damnedest to put the show business back into rock. Her New York Palace
Theatre engagement resulted not only in a personal triumph but an increased awareness on the
part of artists and audiences alike of the still-
unexplored potential for new ways of presenting
pop music. In a year filled with bogus cults, hers
is real and will last"), Landau's review accused
her of "singing so unmusical, so embarrassingly
flat, so brazenly insensitive" that he went on to
suggest maybe the producers were "having a joke
at her expense." His last paragraph concludes,
that being a "musical comedy personality," Bette
needed someone to pick her material—and that
the album proved "beyond a doubt" that Arif
Mardin and Barry Manilow "aren't that someone" and that "she sure as hell can't do it by
herself."

The review alternates between the pompous
and the absurd, as Landau concerns himself more
with clever phrase-making and assorted *ex ca-
thedra* statements (*Rolling Stone* has not become
known as the Pope of Pop for nothing) rather

than relating, in any meaningful or constructive way, to the material or artist that he's dealing with. He follows the old propaganda ploy of *I*-used-to-like-this-person-but-my-*god*-what's-happened-to-her-now? Referring back to his relatively favorable review of the first album seems to give him the right to say anything he likes about this one—as if what he says, because of that earlier "favor," will have some sort of unchallengeable validity, even such broad overstatements as "Bette Midler's recorded performance of 'I Shall Be Released' is the single worst performance of a Bob Dylan song I have ever heard" or generalities like saying the album contains "the artifacts of style without nuance, content or intelligence."

When Bette read the review, Eliot says, her reaction was quiet. "She just sort of looked at it and said, 'How *rude*.' Ben Gillespie was there and he did his best to cheer her up. He kept calling her Betty. He's the only person I know who calls her Betty. But she went into a kind of depression of silence. Later we went out for a walk on Orchard Street. I kept hoping someone would recognize her, ask for an autograph. Finally a clerk in one of the stores did. Then we ended up in a restaurant in Little Italy for dinner, and the waiter was just incredibly nasty to us, saying that we couldn't sit down until the table was cleared. It was just one of those days when everything goes wrong."

8. the gay mystique

defenders and detractors

Bette Midler's early appeal to a largely homosexual male audience seems to have both confused and threatened the straight press, which sought to define that appeal. As recently as late 1978, a writer and editor at the prestigious (but obviously out-to-lunch in terms of contemporary marketing and entertainment trends) *New York Times* opined that Midler got her start "operating on the slimmest base of popular appeal for someone intent on becoming mythological—her adoring audiences were largely homosexual and mostly barely dressed."

Openly anti-gay chauvinism has clouded much of the coverage of Bette's career by the press, including the rock-bottom interview-story by Ed McCormack for *Rolling Stone*. McCormack begins his article with a tongue-in-nose reference to the "crowd of nearly-naked, women-eschewing men" at the Continental Baths, and goes on to call them "hunkering, buggering manmeat herds. Out on the dance floor," he continues, "barely toweled young men enacted a rock-and-roll ritual, dancing like maidens in some primitive puberty rite, while tribal elders overflowed chaises around the pool. It reminded you of a scene of William Burroughs' novel, *The Wild Boys*, in which wild boypacks raised in a womanless society run amok and lay waste to the remnants of Western civilization." McCormack manages to be condescending to a few other oppressed groups (women, orientals, etc.) as well, as he mentions "dark-haired little China dolls in grass skirts" and talks about Bette's "buns" and "disproportionately large bazooms" (disproportionate to what, one can't help but wonder, other than McCormack's own sexual consciousness).

Even writers like Craig Karpel, whose article in *Oui* shows a rather keen understanding of why Bette has such a broad appeal among gays, still find it necessary to sprinkle their copy with derogatory terms, like "fruit" and "fag." And, most writers have felt it necessary to commit themselves (which usually means disapproval) on the question of Bette's gay following. A few have ignored it completely or tried to de-emphasize it (Jon Landau's review of the first album has a classic line in it: "She camps it up with such skill that if her performance is a put-on, that fact is irrelevant"). Even gay writers have felt it necessary to apologize that Midler was campy, or used gay humor—as if those devices were somehow invalid or second-rate in performance. Chief among these detractors has been Arthur Bell, the caustic columnist of *The Village Voice*, who once dismissed Midler rather smugly by calling her "a she imitating a he imitating a she."

Ralph Sepulveda, in another analysis of Midler in *The Village Voice* just before Philharmonic Hall, starts out interestingly by quoting Susan Sontag's "Notes on Camp" (which Karpel does also), but all of a sudden his attitude toward this aspect of Bette's act (and personality, though he doesn't seem to acknowledge that) becomes dismissive: he oversimplifies camp completely by calling "camp sensibility" a "capacity for love of the artificial." Sepulveda is also one of the leading advocates for Bette's "killing off" The Divine Miss M, calling her a "caricature" and "personification of camp" (*Gay*, January 1974) and a detriment to the "real talents" of Bette Midler.

Among all the anti-gay press on Bette, one amazingly positive piece of personal journalism appeared, written by a straight man (rock-writer Richard Goldstein) and appearing (most surprisingly of all) in the publication that more than any other stands for the kind of chic snottiness—*New York* magazine. Goldstein went to the Baths to see Bette (and loved her), but the real confrontation (which he passed on to the readers) was with himself, in the company of McCormack's "hunkering, buggering manmeat herds." Imagine almost any other heterosexual journalist coming to a conclusion like, "But I sometimes wonder whether the limits of my own sexuality aren't really based on the fear of being mocked, turned down or tossed away." Or, "He doesn't look gay. Nobody does. Mostly, they look like me. Men in bath towels or coveralls, or those baggy "Forties trousers, where your basket doesn't show." Or, "But then I start thinking about the number of guys in the room who are touching each other, and how little it means, thinking how much it means when a straight man touches another man, how loaded a gesture that is, even among those of us who believe people *should* touch each other." Ultimately, Goldstein does not feel offended, or superior, or titillated, or defensive. Just a little left out. Nobody offers him a popper (amyl nitrite), and nobody *notices*—at all—when he takes his clothes off and takes a swim in the pool. He walks home with the gay friends he has come with, feeling warm and close to them, but can't help tensing up when one of them puts his arm around his shoulder.

It is not in the least surprising that a performer like Bette Midler could, in part, inspire a piece of journalism as honest and straightforward, as self-revealing as this. Goldstein's article is perhaps the finest example of how important gay liberation —or any personal liberation—is to the whole of society, to the general, uptight status quo. Things are beginning to change, and people like Bette are making that change.

Speaking about the boys at the Baths to Jan Hodenfeld of *The New York Post*, Bette said:

"Essentially, they gave me a big push and we had some good times, but they are still there and I'm constantly moving." The quote got Bette in trouble with a lot of gays: Did this mean she was abandoning them?

The question relates back to the whole question of the makeup of Miss M, and the fact that that character, though very much a part of Bette, is not the whole of her personality—or her talent. It would be reasonable to assume that Bette now feels that she has taken her Baths image as far as it can go. There are new things she'd like to try. They may have an element of camp in them, and they undoubtedly will remain founded in both the sensitivity and outrageousness which gays (and others) found so engaging. But she won't be singing just for gays any more, though she'll always be singing for them, in part. People—at least people like Bette—keep moving; good performers don't get hung up in one category, one style, one audience.

This moving-on does not necessarily denigrate what went before. Bette told Dick Leitsch of *Gay* (January 15, 1973): "As an audience, gay men are spectacular. They're very warm, very responsive. They are the most marvelous audience I've ever had because they're not ashamed to show how they feel about you. They applaud like hell, they scream and carry on, stamp their feet and laugh. I love it." She also stressed to Leitsch that many of her friends were gay: "Being in the theater, one is pretty much surrounded by homosexuality. I really dig it. I laugh and carry on and have a good time. I understand gay guys, I really do. Half the time I think I am one, and I think gay men understand me, too."

Billy Cunningham has said, "Bette's career was manufactured by the New York homosexual society. Let me put it this way: If as much effort and energy had gone into promoting the Gay Rights Bill as went into Bette Midler's career, Arthur Bell could probably be mayor of New York and I would be the treasuress. Because Bette became a cause with homosexuals. It was extremely unfashionable *not* to like Bette Midler. She was a cultural phenomenon. Manufactured by the gay community. But now she's learning that it's not enough to appeal to just a gay audience. Constantly appealing to a gay audience is like constantly running home to Mother. You *know* they're going to love you. It gets to the point where you don't care about anyone else. 'Who cares? My boys love me.' And the terrible thing is that the boys always *do.* Because the boys want to be what she is. It's a wonderful two-way street. The boys want to be that, and the girls love all that adulation."

Gay men have always been a kind of vanguard for women singers (Streisand and Roberta Flack being prime examples of performers whose early club work was for predominantly gay clienteles), and Bette has always acknowledged the force that gays have had on her career. "Bette said that on Chicago television," recalls Bill Hennessy, "some local guy hit her right between the eyes with it, saying, 'You had a big following at the Baths.

Why is it that homosexuals dig you?' Something to that effect. And she said, 'That's always been the case and they have played a very large part in my life, and they certainly did promote me on that level.' "

Bill feels, however, that it is not a level Bette wanted to stay on. "If you think about it, you can go up to Boston, or Washington, and they're still into the drag queen syndrome. Gays like a girl up onstage who's going to be rowdy and noisy, who is going to, in effect, be a kind of drag queen. If you get somebody up there like Sally Eaton or Ellen Greene who *sings*, and presents a pure art form, a lot of them complain, because it's not brassy enough or not loud enough for them. They're still into a lot of 1959 schtick across the country, in the Midwest and all. And that's depressing. Especially when you've seen how gay people other places can really relate to things, to an artist's growth, in terms of sophistication and intelligence."

"Bette hasn't turned her back on gay people," Bill continues. "No way. But on the other hand, she had to sit there in front of nit-picking, thin, screaming queens. All that time. I don't really mean for that to sound derogatory. But they talk about her putting people down. But you should hear *them*. About her. And they know nothing about her. You should hear some of the stories that get back about her. That come out of sheer bitchiness."

Bruce Vilanch mentioned somewhat the same thing. "Bette didn't exploit the gay audience. If anything, they exploited her. They talk about her as if they just got out of bed with her. They all claim to be her best friend. They made her their hero, and then started pretending this familarity with her."

Charlotte says that Bette also got to the point where she resented audiences that were heavily or outrageously gay. "Particularly toward the end of the tour. When she sang 'Am I Blue,' and the second time around, the lyrics say, 'I remember when I was gay,' the audiences would scream and blow whistles. And once she asked them, 'Are you screaming because you like the way I sing the song or because it's got the word 'gay' in it? Well, that's not what the fuck it means. 'Gay' means 'happy.' That song was written at a time when the word 'gay' meant carefree, happy. And now it has a whole other different connotation.' So it did upset her. All that glitter and all that craziness, all those queens being real down, really, really upset her a lot, made her very depressed. And she always kept asking, 'Why, why, why?' And I'd say, 'Honey, those people love you.' And it was hard for her. I saw it. It was difficult for her to overcome that and go on. But she went on anyway. I said, 'It'll be all right. Tomorrow.' It's just a matter of understanding. And being able to draw the line."

"I think she'll always remember her gay following," Charlotte continued. "She can never abandon them, no matter what she does. And she never turned her back on any gay person on a one-to-one basis. She resented gay people only when they were, like, taking over in the audience.

Or the ones who walked up to her and were, like, really, really obnoxious. That's what was depressing. The people who had nothing else in their lives. For whom it was a dead end."

At other times, the gay life style imposed a liberating atmosphere on a performance situation. Sharon Redd sums up, "There are lots of influential gay people in this business. Music, television, theater. And not just men—women, too. There's always that flair, that nice flair. That's what I like about the gayness of the business. It's not that depression you felt when you go into a straight club, and there's a man and woman, and they're drinking, they're trying to get through their life, or whatever, their relationship: they're married or they're living together, or they're trying to break up or trying to cruise somebody over there. With the whole gay thing, there's more an acceptance of one's existence. A happy, up thing. Even though gay life is so transient. There's still an upness about it all. It's almost positive. It's so different, it's just so different. You go into a straight club or a straight environment, and it's always, Well, this is my man and are you looking at him? And there's that smothering and possessing. It makes an atmosphere so uptight. That's why I go to gay clubs most of the time, whether I'm working or not, because I know I can go in there, I can dance by myself, and have a wonderful time—and I'm known for dancing alone, because I have my best times alone. And I don't have to worry, you know. I don't have to worry about somebody looking at me and thinking I'm off my rocker or something. And if I want to dance with a woman, I can dance with a woman without this big, Well, are we gonna make it tonight? Or, Ah, what's this gonna be? Or whatever. It's just so much more relaxed. You know, what you *are* is much more relaxed, I find. So that's why I like it. And I don't mind working for or around gay people, because then I can go into a fantasy that they can understand. More than a straight person can understand."

9. the diva mystique

realizing fantasies

"Why do we perform?" Gail Kantor asked when we spoke of Bette. "Basically because we want to be loved. That's the basic rule of the desire to perform. But, *why*? Why did that happen? There would be different reasons for each person, I guess, and different ways of achieving it. Some people are seeking that love through an honest path, and some people are seeking it by using a lot of artificial means. I think Bette's particular way was a combination of both. She could create a fantasy onstage, but she was always in control of it. She was there to entertain you. She created a character, but it was never completely divorced from *her*, it was sort of an extension of her self. It was complicated in a way, because the reality and fantasy would get all mixed up. She became—she was *determined* to become—a superstar, almost a movie-queen image. It's that determination that makes her different from all the other people around. And Bette *knew* from the beginning, from the Improv or whatever, what she had to do. And she did it. She eliminated barriers for herself by sheer intensity."

In the ideal performance, the wall between audience and performer vanishes. In an almost mystic way, the two sides of the footlights become one. The viewer or listener begins to believe he is actually experiencing what is being related onstage. The *persona*—his star, his diva—becomes his surrogate, linking him to both the pain and joy of this alter-life, which is generally more interesting, more dramatic than his own.

Bette Midler became such a diva only through dreaming the dream first, then realizing that fantasy, carefully and completely. She was able to make herself the vessel for the achievement of the diva mystique because she understood it from the inside, having herself long been a lonely fantasizer—and she remains, even today, an inveterate entertainment-goer, a performer who keeps herself in tune by constantly re-experiencing performance herself, as a member of the audience.

This somehow gives Bette a control over both the mystery and the reality. She can achieve what Jackie Curtis describes as "a sort of haunting" ("It's not necessarily the kind that's frightening or anything. But I can be up there onstage and maybe, although no one can understand what makes a certain expression come over my face, it

A floral tribute for Bette at the Roxy in Hollywood. (Photo by Frank Teti)

Bette during the filming of the concert sequences for *The Rose*. (Photo by Robert Scott)

will make them laugh. Or cry.")—and at the same
time present the fantasy so that even a women's-
lib stalwart is not offended (playwright Myrna
Lamb writes in the August 1973 issue of *Ms.*:
"Her little breast-burdened body is plainly her
conveyance. She rides it out and wheels on all the
fabled female roles: 'Thirties Billie Holiday, all
the Andrews Sisters . . . the lonely little nobody
at the radio, listening to and waiting for the superstar. But the trick is we never forget the superstar
she is waiting for is Bette Midler!").

"I think people who are very involved in life,
who feel complete, do not get involved in cult
followings," says Eliot Hubbard, who was deeply
involved in one of his own once, for Barbra
Streisand (he only recently gave up his fifteen-
pound scrapbook). "I was very lonely, a real
loner. I think cult followings are made up of loners. The loneliness is soothed by the artists.

"I remember the Bon Soir," Eliot continues,
referring to the club where Streisand got her start
(now a rather seedy Latin discotheque). "It was a
real *boîte*. They'd lower the lights, and the main
color was black. The bar was mostly gay. I sort of
wondered why the bar was all men the first few
times I went. Suits and ties, but they packed them
in. Then there were the deuces, tables for two.
The hatcheck girl's name was Lucille and the
doorman was Harry. I went back night after night,
once twelve or fourteen times in a row. Finally,
Barbra asked to see me. 'Why do you come here
every night?' she said. 'Because you sing the songs

different every night,' I replied, very nervously. I think she knew that's what I would say, but just wanted to hear me say it.

"When I went to the Palace and saw all those people waiting at the stage door, I remembered Streisand at the Winter Garden and the Bon Soir. I always considered myself on the outside, watching those who were waiting, but I guess I was waiting, too.

"Certain singers have that cult following and others don't. The ones that do—you simply know are going to be successful. It was the ability that Barbra had to draw me completely out of myself, to be just with her. She was able to create this intimacy, this power. I didn't do anything. I just sat there. It's a power, to single-handedly be able to create this intimacy.

"It was so new to me. I went back night after night. I think it's definitely something that's innate in a performer. It can be polished, made better, but it has to be there to begin with. From what I hear, Bette had it from the beginning, even when she just stood up there with her hands crossed at the Improv."

"Escape is necessary sometimes," Bette told Dick Leitsch of *Gay*, "but always escape heavy. Don't escape into bullshit. Get stoned and listen to Santana. Come to the Baths, the whole world's a baths."

Bette's image of herself as an audience love-object has always been tempered with a clear sense of reality. Though she told Cynthia Spector in *Zoo World* that she wanted to be "a bisexual fantasy . . . the most loved, the most desired woman on this earth," her comment to Neil Appelbaum in *After Dark* would seem closer to the truth: "I want people to love me, but I don't want them to love me for the wrong reasons. Not because I remind them of someone else, but because they see something of themselves in me."

Time (September 10, 1973) quotes Bette as saying: "I just try to have a good time and let the audience in on the secret. It's like giving a party and I am the Grande Hostesse. I always wanted to be Gertrude Stein and have a salon." (The same quote came out in Rona Barrett's *Hollywood Magazine* as wanting "to be Gertrude Stein and have a *saloon*"—which may be equally *a propos*.)

"What I have in me," Bette told Lisa Robinson in *Interview*, "well, it's not hard, and it's not cold, and it's not *fierce ambition*, that's not what it is. It's a drive, but it's not a drive. It's being driven. It's something I have no control over. It's something pushing me, I'm not pushing myself."

Bette's hard-working determination has impressed her friends and audiences (including critics) alike from the beginning. Bill Hennessy and Budd Friedman both describe her as "one of the hardest workers" they've ever known. Michael Goldstein, who dated Bette during the time she was singing at the Improv (prior to the Baths) stresses: "Her tremendous drive to be successful was there at all times. I was in the rock publicity business, and I must admit I didn't foresee the star she was going to be. She was a phenomenal singer even then, but I never dreamed that there would be a marketplace, that people would accept what she was doing in a big way. But *she* believed it. She used to say, 'I'm going to be a great record star,' and I used to say, 'Not in the marketplace of today.' That was the time of Jimi Hendrix and all. But I was wrong. I was totally wrong about that."

Michael Federal points out the importance of that determination onstage: "Bette's incredible. She *fights* to get that audience every night. She's not just techniques. She always *had* to get the audience, otherwise she wasn't happy at the end of the show. She'll do anything she can, just to get a rise out of them. That's what her put-downs were for, even. To get a rise out of the audience. To make them say, Oh, yeah? That's a reaction. That's communication. Then you can say what you want."

Bette's determination also showed through in the way she worked with other people—carefully, professionally. "Bette is a perfect example of a performer who's paid her dues," says Lewis Friedman of Reno Sweeney. "She thought out her performance career carefully, picked the right people. I think that's one of her chief assets. She knows who to work with. Aside from performance, that's her true brilliance, knowing what publicity people to pick, what musicians. She's chosen them just as carefully as she's chosen her material, or her clothes."

The result all adds up onstage. The late Lillian Roxon wrote, following Bette's Philharmonic Hall engagement: "I can't remember when I last saw a performer work so hard and give off and get so much love. I personally happen to think she's very beautiful, but actually her face is both ugly and beautiful, with one facing into the other so you can never quite make up your mind. I watch her hands to see who she really is—they are very slim and graceful and nervously sensitive." (Another performer that Bette greatly admires, Laura Nyro, likewise noted Bette's hands, saying to their mutual friend Peter Dallas, "Bette Midler? You mean the girl with the little, tiny hands? Like a china doll?")

For all Bette's professionalism, in the end it is the "graceful and nervously sensitive" hands that matter most—the honesty and vulnerability beneath all the brassiness, the technique, the trash with flash. "That was something that was just amazing about her," says Michael Federal, "one of the reasons why she got along, one of the reasons why I loved her. There was so much honesty in what she did. Instead of covering herself with things, she used things to open herself up. She's got an incredible knowledge of what things look like onstage—not just how to make things work, but how to *use* a stage. The secret of using a stage is not to cover yourself up, but to *show* yourself. To build a setting in which your own true self shows through. To get your message, the basic truths of what you're trying to say, across. Everything you do onstage is supposed to open that up and make it super-visible, as visible as possible. She used a hundred different things —running around the stage, putting people down, off-the-cuff quips, weird costumes—all those things showed all the different facets of what she was. Not just in themselves. The separate things were even in conflict sometimes—exact opposites. She would get up there and have this crazy costume on and would be running around the stage, and the next thing you knew, she would be sitting down singing something really, really sad. Which sort of turned it around. But she always had that honesty inside her that was showing what she really was. You could call it vulnerability. That's important. Vulnerability. Susceptibility. To an audience that's looking at you. Seeing what you are."

"You make choices in what you do onstage," says Gail Kantor. "Some people say a certain thing is dishonest, and others may not agree. I don't know. I think we've got to stop thinking about it that way. About being honest or dishonest. It's hard to decide, because everything is external. Your body is external. And to use external things as a means to express an internal feeling, it's next to impossible. Anything that you can do with real conviction is not dishonest in my opinion. And when Bette works she does it with complete conviction. There are certain people around who think that they're doing the same thing, but they're not doing it with conviction. It's off the top of their head."

"We're all schizophrenic," says Sharon Redd.

"All of us. I am, I know. We always want to be nice people. And clean. And have clean thoughts. We say we love everyone. When really we may think so-and-so is a bitch. So what Bette would do is come out onstage and she'd read other singers. 'Miss Ice-Cream Karen Carpenter. Goody two-shoes.' And things like that.

"We've been given so many images. Particularly with singers, female singers. They've always presented a certain image. No one had done what Bette did. She was so honest. *Trash*, just out-and-out trash. I mean, what singer would end her show in a slip? She was showing what people really are. Bette gave you real things about real people, instead of some image. For some reason, singers, throughout time, have always presented that sad torch singer who suffers because of her man. No comedy. It's all serious, you know. Either, 'Oh it's a lovely day,' or 'My man has treated me *sooooo* bad.' That place or the other place. Never saying, you know, I need you to fuck me. The way 'Empty Bed Blues' does. Female singers don't just come out and say that. Now they are. Now it's making a change. And I think Bette brought about that change."

Patrick Merla, reviewing Bette's first album in *Saturday Review*, wrote: "On stage Midler seduces audiences into willing complicity by making them identify with her as a person/character as well as a singer/entertainer . . . Midler is an expert comedienne as well as a dramatic actress, with an uncanny ability to 'psych out' audiences and make them love her, almost like Garland. But

Midler reinforces her audiences' belief in their own strength and humanity; she does not play on their bathetic emotions to win them over."

Billy Cunningham says, "It's Bette's ability to internalize whatever she sings that grabs the audience. If you analyze the Bette Midler voice, there's no voice to analyze at all. She's a compilation of a lot of bad things about a lot of good singers. Like the bad parts of Peggy Lee. Or Streisand. Or Chris Connors. She's not their good parts, because if she were their good parts, she would be them. But she *can* internalize whatever she sings, pulling all that beautiful meaning out of the lyrics.

"She doesn't listen to herself sing. And a lot of people do that, listen for their own tones. A lot of people *stop singing* to listen to their own beautiful notes. The note is still coming out of their mouth, but they're not singing any more, they're *listening* to it instead."

Billy also thinks Bette occasionally goes too far. "When she used to do 'Am I Blue' at the Baths, she would actually *whimper* onstage sometimes. And I told her, 'Don't do that. That's awful.' And she said, 'But it moves people.' And I said, 'It does not move people, it embarrasses them. Because you're really *crying.*' You can't really go out there and cry. A person can't empathize musically with something that is that literal. Because that reality is so real, that if you dealt with it yourself, you would go into a state of collapse. You don't deal with it on that level, you internalize it. And use it.

"Bette also has the ability to force you to participate," Billy continues, "and that's a really unique ability. It doesn't mean necessarily that you *like* to participate, it simply means you're forced to participate. You cannot *not* listen to Bette Midler. You can dislike her. But you cannot not listen to her. It's like Barbra Streisand. I don't like Streisand. I never have. But I do not *not* listen to her. Something in the way she sings *compels* me to listen, forces me to deal with the fact that she's singing.

"Whether I'm in a nightclub buying drinks and touching people under the table, or sitting in a theater clutching my program, I am vicariously participating in what I'm seeing, sometimes to the point where I'm actually crying, or actually laughing, or actually hating. I'm so much a part of it that I become it. That's what theater is, and people who don't know that, or who don't know how to deal with that, are not honest people. Or at least they're not dealing with their craft honestly. You can't just go out there onstage and be the thing you are. You've got to go out there and be another whatever-it-is. To be the idea, the thing, the concept."

As Sharon Redd says, "It's characters, you know. Back and forth. It's very schizophrenic, but it helps you in this business. I tell every singer now, find a character. But they say, I want to be honest. But how honest can you be? You know, you commit suicide otherwise."

"I would like to see what is happening in music today combined with a theatrical kind of experience," Bette told Neil Appelbaum in 1971. "That's what I'm shooting for. That's what I'd like to do."

Bette's goal to make pop music dramatic certainly has been achieved. "She's a truly great actress," points out André de Shields. "She knows how to move from one emotional plane or plateau to another. Immediately. With completely smooth transitions. Her face is one of the most believable and instructive masks I've ever seen on a lady on the stage. And it changes constantly. You make those moves with her every time she makes them, and you believe them every time. Many performers have been taught, or have learned, that it's the head that you perform with. That everything happens in the brain, or everything happens in the face. But Bette is one of the few people that I know who works with every cell in her body, and she makes you believe that every inch of her is living, that every inch of her is alive and dedicated to making you completely involved in what she's doing."

Gail Kantor describes Bette as, "Super-dramatic, always conscious of making things work onstage. I'd always notice how she'd curve her back during a slow song like 'Superstar.' She combined acting and singing and dancing, intertwined them all. You can't express one without the other. I really learned a lot from her."

Robin Grean echoes Gail's sentiments even more emphatically. "The two people I've learned the most from are Tom O'Horgan, who directed me in *Jesus Christ Superstar*, and Bette. And if she were ever to go on the road again, or ask me to do anything, I would do it. She's a really remarkable person, and a very disciplined performer. Her way of working reminded me a lot of what I learned from O'Horgan. He used to talk a lot about your *craft*. And it is a craft, and Bette is very aware of that. That's why she goes to concerts and goes to the ballet all the time. She's very disciplined. Incredibly disciplined: She's constantly aware of her craft, and I think I learned a lot from watching her."

"Probably the best remark I ever heard about Bette," says Bruce Vilanch, "came from Ahmet Ertegun, who said, it's the wittiest musical performance he's ever seen. She is all class operating under the guise of classlessness. The classiest, most professional, most sensitive musical act ever. And it probably is. She has unerringly good taste. She picks songs and makes them her own, and she knows what's good. And she has a facility for being able to touch you in so many different ways."

Perhaps it all boils down to the fact that Midler is, first and foremost, an entertainer. All the honesty and artifice, the internals and externals, the talent and determination, the outrageousness and camp eventually add up to that. Bette told Appelbaum: "I believe in entertainment. It has nothing to do with *show business*. It has to do with coming out and throwing vibrations out to an audience and putting them through changes. You know, it's

like making them see in you an experience for
them, that will either change their lives in some
way or perhaps teach them something. I hate that
word *show business*. I don't feel like I'm in show
business. It's more *important* than show business."

"You know what it is about Bette that I think
made everybody love her?" asks Peter Dallas.
"Other performers have told me this. She went
out there and publicly did all the things that people try to cover up. She came out and threw those
things in people's faces. I mean, everybody is insecure when they walk out in front of an audience. Everyone is terrified, no matter how long
they've been doing it. There's just a physical thing
that happens to you before you go out on stage.
And she came out, and instead of trying to cover
it up, she said, 'Oh, honey, I'm such a wreck
tonight. I knew I shouldn't have worn this dress.
It's so tacky.' All the things that performers try to
hide. Performers are supposed to be very together,
they're supposed to have picked the right dress,
they're not supposed to make mistakes. And she
came out and said, 'I'm a mess.' And everyone
could identify with that."

Bette has won the admiration of many of her
fellow performers, from Marlo Thomas to Yoko
Ono ("I like her style. In the age when there is a
question as to what sex comes first, she comes
from that sex which is all sex"—*Ms.*, August 1973)
and choreographer Meredith Monk ("She simply
seems so *real*").

Richard Goldstein, in his piece on the Baths in *New York Magazine*, writes: "I'm shocked, the way I was shocked the first time I saw Hendrix squirting lighter fluid from between his legs, because here is a performer who violates all the proper lovechild rules of rock, the Joplin rule of needful naiveté. Here is the spirit of Tin Pan Alley out there strutting like nobody's business, and the guys in the audience, who have spent a long time sequestering their taste, are seeing the last bastion of true-blue hetero-pop crumble in the face and body and nuance of Bette Midler, who is much more to the point than Alice Cooper, because she's so real-live, so off the wall, and the audience at the Continental knows her and honors her because they know she is Right."

Bruce Vilanch states: "Like all great performers, what Bette does is touch everybody in a different way. And she does this in a way that very few people have ever done. Bette, probably more than any performer in the history of show business, draws upon every single tradition. She draws on music from every decade. She draws on show-biz gimmicks of every kind. And all the different walks of life that she takes her characters from. And as a result she's going to hit everybody a different way. You're going to have somebody that's going to sit there and hear 'In the Mood' and 'Boogie Woogie Bugle Boy' and say, 'Fabulous, I love it.' Or the shoulder pads. Or the flower in her hair. Or the platform shoes. And somebody else is going to say, 'God, I wish she would can that shit, why doesn't she just shut up and sing? Kurt Weill and songs like that? Hoagy Carmichael and Johnny Mercer.' And then you get someone like Jon Landau who says her real value is that she recasts the great rock songs like 'Do You Want to Dance' and 'Uptown,' and she brings out the beauty in them that was always there. And then you're going to get someone like Ellen Willis, who thinks that Bette's the great feminist of all time because she's commenting on the roles that we play, and the artificiality of these roles.

"When you touch someone in so many different ways, and touch so many people in so many different ways, there's no way that you can avoid making some of them unhappy. And so you get somebody like Arthur Bell, saying, 'I think her talent is great, but I can't stand her act.' Saying the Divine Miss M must go, give us Bette Midler. Jon Landau says that, too. And neither of them, in my estimation, understands what she's doing onstage. But they're both moved by something that she does, nonetheless, in spite of the fact that they don't understand it. They're moved by another element of it. And that's the mark of a great performer. There just aren't any other performers who do that, who touch everybody. It's incredible."

Craig Karpel writes: "Bette Midler has chosen to perform examples from as many genres of material as there are varieties of musical taste among her potential audience . . . she diversifies, she appeals to a spectrum of audiences simultaneously. She doesn't put all her eggs in one basket . . . but rather, figures out how many baskets there are altogether and allocates an egg here, two eggs there, one over *there*, let's see, have we forgotten anybody?"

"I would rather hear her belch in an elevator shaft," Karpel continues, "than hear Carly Simon whining about clouds in her goddamned coffee or—angels and ministers of grace defend us! —Helen Reddy warbling invincibly about she is Woman, watch her grow, watch her singing toe to toe."

"She was very, very determined." Bill Hennessy sums up: "To prove it to *them*. To shove it in their faces. She worked on that level, and as a result that challenge, that proving ground for her, was what spurred her on, what brought her to the heights. It was a kind of anger almost. Now that the anger is gone, now that she's proved that, is why it's so difficult for her to go on to the next place."

10. the next place

making the move to movies

It's been apparent to all Midler-watchers (including Bette and Aaron) for some time that the "next place" that Bill Hennessy was talking about had to be movies. Since the days of the Palace, Russo and Bette had been reading and rejecting scripts, looking for the right vehicle. Among the roles allegedly nixed for Midler's screen debut were the Barbara Harris role in *Nashville*, the Talia Shire role in *Rocky*, and the Stockard Channing role in Mike Nichols's *The Fortune*.

There are rumors that Bette insulted Nichols when they met to discuss the script—by asking him what he'd "done lately"—but Candy Leigh recalls, "Aaron didn't think it would be a success" (it wasn't) "and Bette was unhappy with the woman being ridiculed throughout. She wanted to change the end so the woman won out over the man. She and Nichols, of course, did not agree."

During this period between the Palace and the Minskoff, Leigh recalls Russo and Bette reading many, many scripts: "Scripts arrived almost daily. It took a long time because, in my opinion, Bette suffered the same dilemma most serious actresses have—finding a script that treats a woman with dignity and intelligence. Also, because her career as a concert performer and recording artist had been such an unprecedented success, she had to be especially cautious in her choices."

Bette also at one point very much wanted to portray Dorothy Parker's life story on the screen, a role she would seem to be a natural for. Screen bios of Sophie Tucker and Texas Guinan were also discussed.

Bette told Craig Zadan at the time of his *New York* magazine piece in 1975: "The one we really wanted was the film version of *Little Me*. Now, we lost that one under very unusual circumstances. It all goes back to when Ross Hunter's *Lost Horizon* came out. Well, my dear, they threw us out of the theater, we were laughing so hard. I *never* miss a Liv Ullmann musical. Well, anyway, Ross Hunter was very insulted. Aaron's not one to mince words, and when he met Ross Hunter about another project, Aaron said something to him about questioning his judgment because he thought '*Lost Her-Reason*' was abominable. Well, word got out that we were after *Little Me*, and wouldn't you know it, Hunter went out and bought it for Goldie Hawn."

Broadway musical roles were turned down as well during this whole period (including such losers as *Rachael Lily Rosenbloom* and *Mack & Mabel*), but Bette has always maintained she would like to act seriously on stage. Candy says, "She projected eventually retiring to London to perform with a repertory company." And Bette told Stan Mieses of the *Daily News*: "I'd like to become a great actress—there, it's out. I started that way, you know. I studied with Strasberg—I didn't understand a blinking thing. They had no sense of humor. And I've learned a lot since." She also told Mieses that she would love to do "a comedy full of whimsy," and in an interview with William Sherman she added: "I would luuuuve to do Noël Coward on Broadway. I'd kill to do Noël Coward."

But Midler is quite adamant about not doing anything if it doesn't seem "right" to her. "I just don't want to do garbage," she told Gerrit Henry. "What a lot of people don't know about me, though, is that I am an extremely moral person. I believe in home, security, love, all the good things. But I also believe in having a good time on stage. I think you've got to have the fun, the bawdiness, the put-downs, to strip away the show-business sentimentality and get down to home truths."

Meanwhile, Midler's been doing lots of home-work. She's always been a movie freak, as was apparent when she spoke to Lisa Robinson in *Interview* early in her career. When Robinson asked her if she had seen Rita Hayworth in *Gilda* on television, Midler replied: "Of course. I saw it for about the fifth time. She was so gorgeous. A lot of those women were breathtaking. Dolores Del Rio would make you gasp. Dolores Del Rio when she was young. I couldn't believe such a person existed."

Candy Leigh recalls: "During the period that I worked with her, an unknown actor named Robert De Niro made a film called *Mean Streets*. Bette was one of the first people to see it and was completely taken with the film and, even more so, with De Niro's performance. She spoke so frequently and so passionately about his work that I went out of my way to see what was still an obscure film. She was right."

Midler told William Sherman in an interview for the *Daily News* prior to the Copa engagement: "Did you see *Saturday Night Fever*? I haaaated it. It's exploitive of women. Absolutely. That is not Brooklyn. The men were too piggish. And did you ever see a dancer in a leotard with high heels? John Travolta, too. He was exploited. He's a nice guy. It's too bad."

Bette's interest in movies and theater is equalled by her passion for dance and ballet. She was very disappointed when a musicians' strike caused the cancellation of her planned appearance as guest performer with one of her favorite dance companies, the New York City Ballet. She was to take the acting-speaking role (no dancing) in a revival of George Balanchine's *The Seven*

Deadly Sins—the role Lotte Lenya had played in the 1933 original.

Principal shooting on *The Rose* was completed in mid-1978, but the film is not scheduled for release until late 1979. A few clips were shown along with a Midler interview on the *Up Close* series on Home Box Office. Midler has turned her red hair honey-blonde and she looks good—as does the film, judging by the clips. The performance bursts with intensity, and the screaming rock voice sounds terrific (much better than Midler's voice has in a long, long time).

A European tour in late 1978 seems to have been primarily to pre-hype the movie in that area. The Harlettes did not go along, though Ula went to Los Angeles to drill the trio who did accompany Bette in some of the old routines. ("They were all white," she recalls. "*Extremely* white. They sounded—well, a couple of them once backed Bob Dylan, so that sort of shows you. They filled out our outfits very well, though. They definitely had big tits.")

20th Century–Fox is reported to have spent nine million dollars on *The Rose*, which was finally directed by Mark Rydell (after reportedly going through four other directors). In it, Alan Bates plays the rock singer's manager, and the fact that Bates is made to look a lot like Russo leads one to wonder how much the screenplay has been changed to incorporate Bette's own experiences in the music industry.

Sharon Redd recalls that during the Copa tour, "There was a script that they were all working on —Bette, Aaron, Jerry Blatt. Everyone on the tour was in it. Hairdressers, road managers, back-up singers, the whole bunch. Which is what they've done with the movie, I guess. It's not really about Janis anymore. Although Bette herself was a real Janis Joplin fan. She really idolized Janis."

At the time of the Copa, when the film was being directed by someone named Larry Peerce, Midler told William Sherman that, after all this time of searching for the right role, "This is it. It's about a blues singer. Not just Janis Joplin, but a combination of all those stars of the '60s. Jim Morrison, too."

What next? The reports from the studio are very promising. Warren Hoge of *The New York Times* reported: "Studio viewers, watching the dailies as the 14-week shooting schedule came to an end this summer, had little doubt that Midler can be a compelling screen actress. There is not a detractor among the cast and crew, a group not always given to generosity in receiving an un-proven leading lady in its midst."

There are other projects already in the works, according to Hoge, which include a situation comedy set in Las Vegas (for United Artists), plans for a remake of the musical *Gypsy*, and a movie biography of early feminist/socialist "Red Emma" Goldman.

Whatever happens now, Bette Midler has taken the plunge she's always wanted to make, into the

Hollywood pool—and without Aaron Russo still paddling around as her "self-appointed Louis B. Mayer" (as Charlotte puts it).

Now it's time to sink or swim.

11. home to myself

realizing realities

Isn't camp wonderful? Tomorrow we have archery and horseback-riding.
—Overheard at the Improvisation

So what is Bette Midler *really* like? She picks up litter on the streets and once told a reporter she would like to be sanitation commissioner of New York City. She disapproves of gambling. Steve Ostrow once called her a prude to *Rolling Stone*. She doesn't like crowded rooms. She and Michael Federal used to go horseback-riding. She avoids big-name fashion designers because she doesn't want to "get lumped with all those idle women, the women kind of women." Money makes her nervous. She quit analysis after a year because she had better ways to spend her money. As to sexual and international politics, she's pro-abortion, pro-peace anti-violence, and opposes role-playing or bigotry on any level. She's supportive of her friends in the entertainment industry, but not too fond of hangers-on and people who try to assume familiarity with her. She's a private person and rather dislikes being in the public spotlight, except when she chooses to step into it. She's an incognito schlepper, always going and doing. She's Bette Midler and the Divine Miss M, at one and the same time, and the last thing she'll ever be is simple to understand or categorize.

"I am the schizophrenic that you see, with all those little personalities," *Playboy* quotes Bette as saying. London rock writer Roy Hollingworth says she told him, "This is me, and that divine lady up on stage is me too, baby. I like them both a whole lot, and I miss each of them when I'm without the other."

"Miss M is both a drawback and an asset," Bette told Loraine Alterman in an interview that appeared in *Record World* and *Ms.* in 1973. "When I started and was doing Miss M, I was hiding. I still hide to a certain degree because it's really painful to get up and expose yourself to people. It killed Janis Joplin. I have found recently that I don't have to hide any more. Last summer's Schaefer Concert in Central Park was a real knockout for me. I was dressed very normally. That was really the happiest night of my life because I found out that I didn't have to hide, that they would take me for what I was, that I had succeeded and that I had achieved what I had started out to achieve, which was to come to myself, to come back to Bette Midler. I know now that I can take people on a theatrical adventure or I can take them on a musical adventure or I can take them on an encounter group. Once you can eliminate the fear that you can't do it, then you are free. And I'm very nearly free."

Bette's liberating effect as a performer has stemmed directly from her own personal liberation, from discovering a strong sense of self, one that led to a considerable degree of self-knowledge and self-respect. Asked by May Okun of the New York *Daily News* if she had considered getting a nose job, Bette replied negatively, adding: "I'd be real embarrassed if people knew that I did it . . . To me altering the way you look goes somewhere else, it's a whole other realm of thought. I always thought strangely about people who have altered themselves."

She told Alterman: "Every two minutes you turn around, there is someone else that will tell you that this is what you have to buy, this is the deodorant you have to use in order to be accepted and presentable and loved. Some women spend their whole lives doing nothing but trying to keep up with that. I was hoodwinked into it myself, but somewhere along the line it took a perverse turn. Somewhere along the line the perspective changed. I became more sure of myself as a person when I took the anti-advertising stand and decided I wouldn't let them tell me what personality to have. When I decided that I didn't want to look the way they wanted me to look and decided that I would look exactly the opposite way and do it just the opposite way they were telling me to do it. That's when I took control of my own destiny and that's when the success started happening."

On the women's question, Bette told Dick Leitsch of *Gay*: "I do find role-playing a problem sometimes. I like being a woman, but I don't like being a stereotype of a woman. I have my diaphragm and I do what I can do."

Arguments go on and on in the will-the-real-Bette-Midler-please-stand-up sweepstakes:

Billy Cunningham: "Bette was always the same. Whether she was wearing a gown or whether she was wearing bluejeans. I've talked to Bette at nine-thirty in the morning when she could barely speak English, and she was just as crazy then, just as nonsensical as when I went to see her at night at work. There is no Divine Miss M. There's just Bette."

Bill Hennessy: "She's very different offstage. Everyone who sees the Divine Miss M thinks they're seeing Bette, but that's only a touch of her. As an artist, she's a very private human being, very private, very academic. She enjoys reading, enjoys going to school, and she enjoys learning. She's very compassionate—very much a Jewish-mother type without being a Jewish-mother type. She's a very, very private, shy person. She likes things quiet. She likes to go into clubs very unobtrusively. She is not one of *these people*. I don't think she's like Liza Minnelli at all, running around with the crowd, or the East Side Halstons,

Bette during the filming of the concert sequences for *The Rose*. (Photo by Robert Scott)

The End

(Photo by Robert Morris)

and all that. Just a very dedicated, artistic human being."

Michael Federal (quoted in *Rolling Stone*): "She's a very fiery lady. She's always rushing somewhere, but she's never there on time."

Charlotte Crossley: "Bette's a Sagittarius, with her moon in Scorpio, Aries rising. Which makes her—well, the fire and the water are in constant conflict with each other. The Scorpio is the thing that makes her kind of flowing, but it can also make her very very poisonous. I'm sure you've heard rumors, heard things about her temper."

Bette (*New York Post*): "I am a very, very strong woman—Sagittarius with Aries rising, a Scorpio moon and lots of Leo—almost completely a fire chart."

Robin Adams Sloan's Gossip Column, New York *Sunday News*, June 23, 1974: "What is singer Bette Midler like offstage? Pretty much the prima donna. She really believes her little name-tag—the Divine Miss M, and friends think that the sudden bash of fame has gone to her pretty little head. Some associates swear they'll never work for her again. Miss M even had the nerve to offer a well-established singer a job with her back-up group."

Bette (in *Interview*): "I would go to [Steve Paul's early '60s rock club] The Scene, and I would hide—way in the background. I was always frightened. To get up in front of the audience at The Scene, that would have been very hard for me. I would have been really scared, because at that place, everyone was attitudes, I mean it was attitudes forever, and I can't attitude. I just can't do it, I'm a Sagittarius, and very blunt, and I can't put attitudes on. I can see when someone else is doing it, and if there was someone watching me do it I would be terrifically embarrassed."

"I could always go yadda-yadda with her," says Charlotte Crossley of her relationship with Bette. "We have some kind of connection, closeness. Bette and I really got to be chums. She was always asking me what I thought of this and that, and I would always give her my 'T'—what I thought, or what I'd heard about this and that and the other. And she'd go, 'Charlo!' And I'd always tell her about really decadent, really sleazy things. And she'd go—she's actually kind of naive about some things—she'd go, 'Things aren't really like that, are they?' And I'd go, 'Yes they are, they're really like that.'"

Linda Hopkins met Bette while Linda was on Broadway in the musical *Purlie*, for which Bill Hennessy was hairdresser (the same position that he had had in *Fiddler* when he first met Bette). Linda recalls: "Bette used to come backstage and to our dressing rooms and sit and rap with everybody. And somehow or another Bette and I managed to get really close. As friends. And then we started following one another around. You know, wherever she'd work, I'd come, and wherever I'd work, she'd go. And it's still like that. We keep up with one another.

"You know, the way I'd describe Bette's personality in life is like, God, she's always happy-go-lucky. In other words, if you were miserable

yourself or you had something on your mind, and
you got around Bette, you might as well forget it,
because she wasn't gonna dare allow you to be
sad or have your head hung down low. Bette is a
person, well, she always feels like she's a philosopher, you know. 'Okay, all right, you got problems, tell 'em to me, and I'll listen.' And she
listened. She will listen to what you have to say.
But if she thinks that you're having pity for yourself, then, man, watch out. She don't allow that.
She don't believe in pity. 'If you want to be that
way, all right, but put your own self down that
drain. But if you mean anything to yourself, you
know, turn that drain loose. Put a cover over that
drain. And walk away.' I remember her saying
that to me once, because I was down once. And
when Bette finished talking *about* me, I got up
right away. It helped. She's like a psychologist.

"Whenever I got ready to sing my song—I was
the church soloist in *Purlie* and I had the opening
song in the show—Bette would always make sure
that she would be there so that she could catch
me. And it used to make me feel great, seeing her
standing there in the wings. 'Cause I always knew
that Bette, you know, she hadn't made it then, she
was still just like struggling then. But I always
knew something about her, that she would make
it. Because, you see, Bette Midler, she don't believe in nothing but 'whatever *you* believe in, go
get it.' So whenever I'd see her out there, she'd be
cocking her finger and telling me, 'Go, sing it for
me.'

"One time I was really hoarse and I really

really didn't think I could make it, and my understudy said, 'Do you want me to go on for you?' And Bette said, 'What the devil are you talking about?' She said, 'You go right out there and do it yourself. Nobody is supposed to know that you're hoarse out on that stage.' And I looked at her, and I said, 'Okay.' I said, 'All right.' I said, 'I'm gonna do it, but I don't know how I'm gonna make out.' She said, 'You're gonna do it, if you *know* that you're gonna do it. But if you feel you're not going to do it, dummy, stay off the stage. And by then, I was just *resentful*. And when I got out there and made that high note clear as a whistle, she just fell out. I came off and she said, 'Thanks, dummy.' "

When Linda played Reno Sweeney in the spring of 1974, Bette showed up the third night and jammed with her until the wee hours of the morning. "After the show," Linda says, "the place closed and everybody had left. They closed the doors, and there was Bette and I still sittin' in there. So we went into our own little jam session. They just let Bette and I and her company stay in. We got to singin' till after four o'clock in the morning, just the two of us. I was playin' the piano, and she was singin' and I was singin'. And when we finished singin', we looked at one another, and we started cryin'. And huggin'. Cause we was happy that one another had made it, that we'd got a foothold on the ground, you know. No more strugglin', like. We cried like two babies.

"Bette Midler is, honest before God, you'll never find another person like Bette Midler. I don't care how big Bette Midler is, and right now she's just as big as Liza or anybody else, but she's still Bette Midler, she still remembers where the back door is, she would never climb above that. Not Bette.

"I tell you. To me, there's four people in this business that really maintain what they had after they made it big. That's Liza Minnelli, Gladys Knight, Melba Moore, and Bette Midler. I call them all my children. I just adopted them all. And they really like boss me, because if they tell me to do something, I do it. I obey them, because I love them. Bette and I hangs out together more. When we see one another, we don't care what time we get home. And Liza's the same way. And Leslie Uggams, I can't leave her out. Good performers don't ever change. They stay the same. They stay humble. It's the ones that have been pushed up there that are the ones that are afraid to be themselves."

When a benefit was held at Reno Sweeney for Holly Woodlawn's bail fund (the transvestite performer had gotten into trouble with the law on a forgery charge), Bette and Aaron were there, arriving late and sitting quietly at the end of the bar. Before leaving they each unobtrusively slipped Reno's manager Buddy Fox a check for the fund. "That was significant, I think," Buddy says, "because it shows that Bette realized how important Holly is as a *conceptual* figure on the music scene today, whether you want to call it glitter rock or whatever."

Such stories seem to disprove the contention in

some quarters that Bette has abandoned her old
friends, or has "changed" with her success. "I
don't believe Bette has cut herself off," says Bill
Hennessy, "from me or anyone, really. We're still
friendly. It's the tightness it once was, but it's a
different relationship now. It's not me going out
with her, no, it's a totally different relationship.
But she has tremendous respect for me. She's
come to see my groups. She's very happy where
I'm at. A lot of people used to say, 'Well, you've
been fucked—she really screwed you,' and all that.
But, bullshit, no way. Bette hasn't screwed me. On
the other hand, without her, without that preface,
I would not be where I'm at today. That's a reality. Neither would Barry. Or a lot of other people.

"I think there are ways of dropping people, like
Streisand is supposed to drop people by simply
denying their existence in her life. That to me is
cruel. I don't like her, and the little I've heard
about her makes me think she's a very cold, mean
lady. But on the other hand, there's a way to
soften the blow. Like Bette does.

"People simply grow apart. Move in separate
directions. I don't see eighty-five percent of the
people I used to know eight years ago. How could
I? I was a hairdresser eight years ago. I couldn't
possibly. I mean, I've changed so radically.

"But people, performers especially, move on in
this business. And sometimes you step on people's
toes by accident in the process. There's nothing
you can do about it."

Patrick Cochrane, who was her secretary the
last four months before she left New York City

for California, says that offstage "Bette was real quiet, real shy, but very pleasant. She likes to go to a few shows and all, but she doesn't see people much, doesn't have a lot of friends. She reads everything, and she sleeps a lot. Does things like teaching herself French. But she's basically not very exciting offstage.

"As far as business goes," Patrick continues, "she used to do most of it over the phone or through Aaron. She's very Rolodex oriented.

"She was also very clean. Washed the tub every time she bathed. With Comet."

Just how private a person Midler was was driven home to Cochrane by a statement she made about his predecessor as her secretary: "His biggest mistake was he thought we were friends."

This insistence on privacy is mentioned frequently by those who have been acquainted with Bette. "I don't really know her," says Gail Kantor, who has stayed rather friendly with Bette since dropping out as a Harlette. "There was proximity, but I never got to be really *close*. Even though we had very similar backgrounds and all."

"Bette's a very immediate person," adds Robin Grean. "Very concerned with what's happening now. And, especially if she's working, she's concerned about the performance *that* night. I don't think she thinks very far ahead. She does not think years ahead, or even months and months ahead. And I don't think she really looks back a great deal, either. I think to her, it's all a part of her. But the thing is just to continue moving on."

One person who did feel snubbed by Bette in her newfound success was Budd Friedman, who had given her her first club exposure at the Improvisation and also became her first manager. Friedman reacted negatively to all the hoopla that came out in the press about Bette getting her start at the Baths. "That was a crock of shit. And I was very upset, over the years about all that publicity, with no mention of the Improv. And I bumped into Bette at a luncheon at the St. Regis, for Geraldo Rivera or someone, and I just let her have it. Cursed her out for about three minutes. She started crying and everything. It was really quite a scene."

Budd and Bette made their peace just before the Palace opening, and she went to the Improv after the show opening night. "And when I saw her at the Palace," Budd says, "I was sitting up there in the mezzanine, watching the show very carefully, judging it, you know, because I was pretty familiar with most of the stuff that she was doing. Then she came out with a line that I hadn't heard before, and I just guffawed—really let go a laugh, and she stopped and said, 'Is that Budd Friedman's laugh? I know that laugh. He was my first manager. He's a terrible man, but he owns a great club over on the West Side. West 44th Street.' Hysterical."

"I love to be in love," Bette told May Okun of the *New York News Magazine.* "I'm always very happy and I do my best work when I'm in love. But I happen to have a lot of trouble with relationships . . . I'm really a child of the media and I always believed those stories, those images in the movies and on TV. That's why I do what I do when I get involved with people, and it doesn't seem to work. I figured all that stuff was drawn from life, and now I can't figure out why life isn't like that. So now I'm trying to unlearn those lies, and find out what the truth is."

Despite Ed McCormack's crack in *Rolling Stone* that offstage Bette "looks like a girl who doesn't get asked out on Saturday night," Bette's name has been linked romantically with a number of people: Ben Gillespie, Michael Federal, Luther Rix, Aaron Russo, Trip Cale (her sound man on the tour that took her to the Palace), and, most recently, actor Peter Reigert, one of the stars of the movie *Animal House*, whom she met in New York while he was appearing off-Broadway in a show called *Sexual Perversity in Chicago*. ("She went backstage to meet him after the show," says Sharon Redd, "and he asked her out to dinner. It's been a love story ever since.")

"I bequeath to you those towers," Bette told Peter Dallas on turning over to him the keys of her apartment on West 75th Street (referring to the towers of the San Remo, a large residential hotel visible against the Central Park skyline through the windows of the front room). "Those towers will hold you up, Dallas, whenever you're down."

Dallas, who had become friendly with Bette during the early days at the Baths, had in turn found Bette a new apartment in the Village when she told him she wanted a larger place, but couldn't hunt for one herself because she was busy with her first album. "She said, 'I want something very special and very charming.' So I found her something very special and very charming. In a landmark building, which will never be torn down. With a real fireplace and a backyard.

"Here," said Dallas, indicating the old apartment, "she lived in the bedroom mostly. She worked in the front room, though, and had a couple of plants hanging around. But that was about it. Except for this funky old armchair. I mean, this chair was a hundred years old, the springs were all popped out and lying on the floor. She was going to throw it away, but I begged her for it. And hung on to it long after its death. Until finally, there was *nothing* more to cover it with."

Speaking of her Barrow Street apartment, Bette said to Chris Chase: "The place likes me. I knew as soon as I walked in the door it was glad to have someone there. I'm trying to make it comfortable, like a home. I've never really had a home. I lived in one place for five years, but I had no furniture. I had a rug on the floor and I had some mattresses."

Charlotte says, "Bette wants to be a regular little person, in her little home, her little apartment. And grow her plants. She wants to be a regular person. As unpretentious as possible. She wants to be domestic. I don't think she looks upon herself as a star at all. Even though she knows she's a diva among divas."

"I don't really pay too much attention to the signs of success," Bette told May Okun. "The people screaming. It's very dangerous to believe all the things they say about you . . . it's not the truth, it's not everyday life.

"I did it all for my own satisfaction," Bette continued, "to see if I could do it. To see if anyone could understand it if I put it in front of them, to see if there was anyone else out there who was dreaming the same dreams I was dreaming."

Bette also told Okun that she had felt no real identity crisis in her career: "I knew who I was and I knew what I was going to do. Now I'm getting to the point where I'm almost finished doing it."

Bette has made other hints to the press that now, since she has done what she set out to do, in terms of a particular musical image (or collection of images), she may either retire or move on to something else. She clearly has no desire to repeat herself.

"If the crap started growing around me," Bette told Roy Hollingworth, "if it all became too big, then I would just go back to my little circle of clubs and friends, and be very happy to go back. I have a lot of friends."

Reminiscing about the time she sang "God Bless the Child" at Hilly's (the awakening that led her to really seriously pursue her singing career),

Bette told Al Rudis of the *Chicago Sun-Times*: "I had an experience, some kind of breakthrough. And when I came out at the end I knew I had to do that. For as long as the trip will be, I had to live it out." And Paul Gardner, writing from Hollywood for *The New York Times*, quotes Bette as saying (jokingly, according to the reporter), "I have a few more musical statements to make before I leave my public."

Affecting people is important to Bette (she told Lisa Robinson: "That's really a turn-on, to see all those people being different from one another and getting along . . . and not see them spitting at each other, even if it's for an hour and a half or so . . . that's really nice"), but the whole superstar, social-climbing trip seems to interest her very little—in herself or others.

Charlotte says: "You meet all these people and you remember what you read about them in the fan magazines. And you realize they're just people. But there's a whole pretentiousness that I just can't cut. The Hollywood thing was just too much. I was ready to jump off the Hollywood sign. I went into a bar with Bill out there. And there were all these people. This guy from a big television show, giving you tanner than tan, coiffed-er than coiffed, hair in place, with some cheese-bomb-looking babe. And there were a lot of other very pretentious types in there, and I couldn't stand it. After a while being in Hollywood, you get used to their attitudes, I guess, 'cause everybody's a star out there—gas attendants and the

people who park cars. Everyone. They're all, like,
you know, aspiring."

Charlotte also describes a night that she saw
Bette at Reno Sweeney. They were both there to
hear Bruce Vilanch. "I was there, and all of a
sudden Bette walked into the room and the karma
got incredibly heavy. Everybody else's—not
Bette's. Everybody else became very aware that
she was in the room. And that this one was sitting
with her, or that one was sitting with her. All
these assholes were sitting with her and being very
today, very small-mouthed, you know? I was
there, with Barry and some people. I talked with
Bette, and we dished some, but I didn't want to sit
there with her, because of all those pretentious
people around her. I mean, after a while it gets so
pretentious you just can't stand it any more. I
mean these people—their cheeks are so sucked in
and they've got so much Aramis Bronza on, that
they can't even talk to you."

"It's really, really lonely at the top," Charlotte
continues. "I guess that's why I wouldn't want to
go there. And that's Bette's biggest fear. Being
alone. And I find that she's very lonely. But I'm
sure she'll never go the way of Marilyn, or go the
way of Billie. She'll live to see her success and to
enjoy her success. But there's an inner happiness
and an inner peace that she is searching for. I
know that, and I've heard her say that, and it's not
so much in other people that she's got to find it,
as in herself. That's where she's got to find it and
realize it. And she knows that. 'Sometimes I'm

good,' she says, 'and other times, I'm not so good.' "

Bette Midler is a liberator, an iconoclast, an entertainer, a great interpreter of songs and styles, of music, lyrics, and life. Most importantly of all, she has given her audience and her associates the exceptional sense of self that she, in her own life and career, has discovered. .

Gail Kantor seems to have discerned the complexity and significance of this sense of self more than anyone else I encountered in talking to people about Bette Midler:

"We had just gotten back from a gig in Philadelphia. It was the first night of Passover, December 1972, and my parents invited Bette and Aaron, and a friend of mine named Bob, over to their house in Brooklyn for Seder. It was a very strange evening. My uncle and aunt were there, and my parents, but not my brothers, who were out of town.

"Seder was really terrible, just awful. There was no joy in it. Everyone was being really natural and everything. And my parents liked Bette. But afterwards, after dinner, we got into this whole talk about bigotry. My father at the time was recovering from a heart attack. A mild one, but we didn't want to get him excited. And I started getting crazy inside. You know, I wanted to scream and cry and everything all at once. I wanted to throw a tantrum.

"And Bette saw it happening, and she said, 'Gunindl—she always called me Gunindl—'just calm down.' She understood, because she goes through the same thing with her father. The same relentless pursuit of trying to be *heard*. The frustration of 'Listen to me! It's not only what you're saying that counts. Listen to me. Get my words in your soul.' And, you know how it is. My parents mean well and everything. They're the kind of people who don't really want to sacrifice their beliefs. They've become so ingrained that it's hard for them to understand anyone else's beliefs—to get behind the words. Especially when it comes to talking about reality, about people. My mode of life is undoubtedly something they can't understand. They respect me, but they don't understand it.

"And here were my two worlds clashing. Here I was with three people who were typical of the people that I live among, in my day-to-day life. Very emotional people. Who work around vibrations, more than intellect. Although they have intellect. But who *feel* things. And listen. Who are basically open, which the people I come from are not. I mean my parents have difficulty functioning in that natural way that the people I live with do. And I put myself in a very heavy situation that night. And Bette really calmed me down.

"The last year before I started working with Bette was a very big growth period for me. It was not spurred on by the Bette Midler experience, but it was enhanced by it. And my relinquishing my past, my saying, 'Gail, all right, you're nobody else, you've got to be what you are and you've got to do what you do.' I started accepting my self more readily. And that's when this whole period began. It was just a whole wonderful new experience to do that trip, the Bette Midler trip."